That Balance So Rare

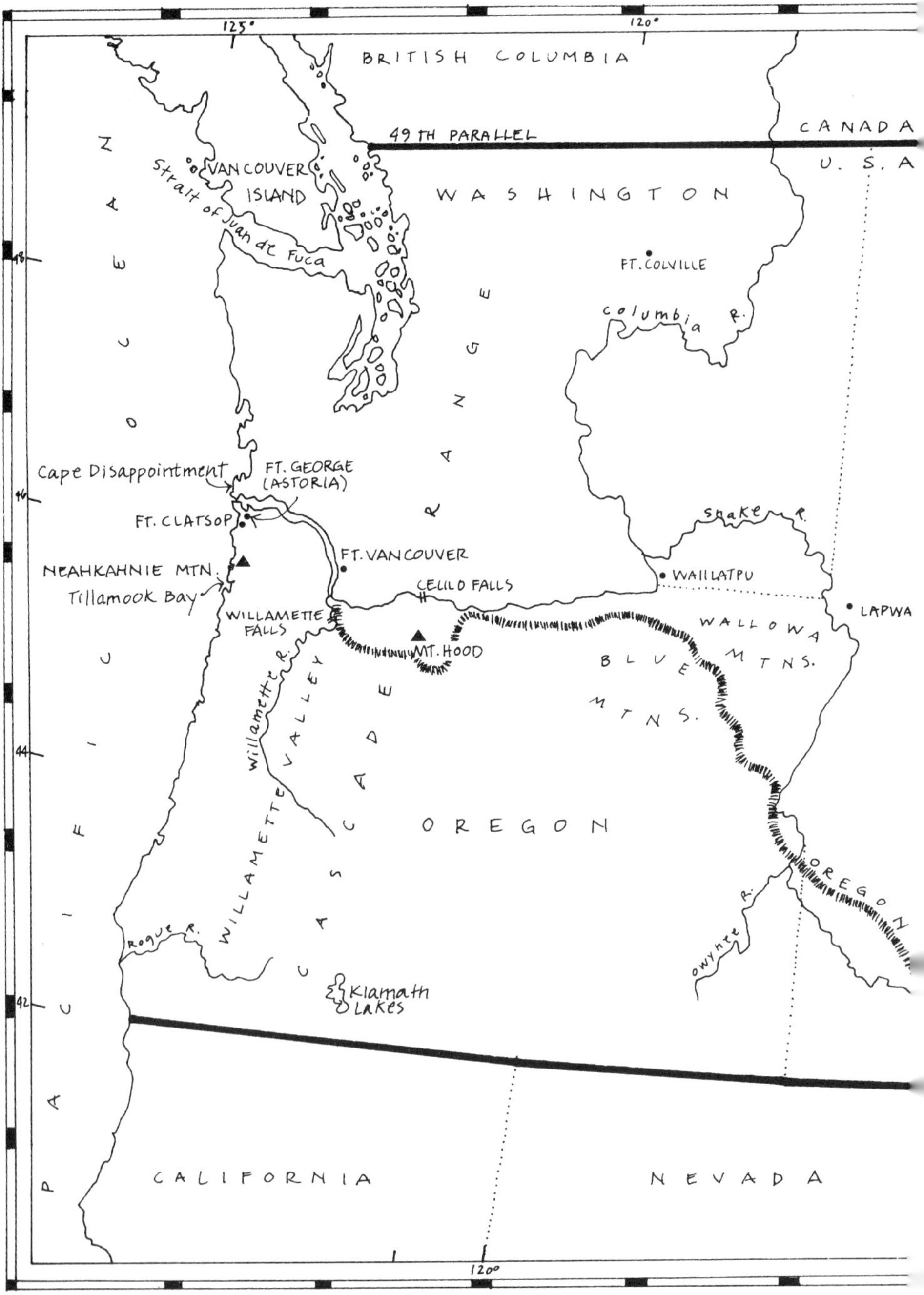

BRITISH COLUMBIA

125° 120°

49 TH PARALLEL

CANADA
U.S.A

VANCOUVER
ISLAND

Strait of Juan de Fuca

WASHINGTON

FT. COLVILLE

Columbia R.

48

Cape Disappointment

FT. GEORGE
(ASTORIA)

FT. CLATSOP

46

Snake R.

FT. VANCOUVER

WAIILATPU

LAPWA

NEAHKAHNIE MTN.

CELILO FALLS

WALLOWA
MTNS.

Tillamook Bay

WILLAMETTE
FALLS

MT. HOOD

BLUE

MTNS.

Willamette R.

CASCADE

RANGE

44

WILLAMETTE VALLEY

OREGON

OREGON

Owyhee R.

Rogue R.

42

Klamath
Lakes

CALIFORNIA

NEVADA

PACIFIC OCEAN

120°

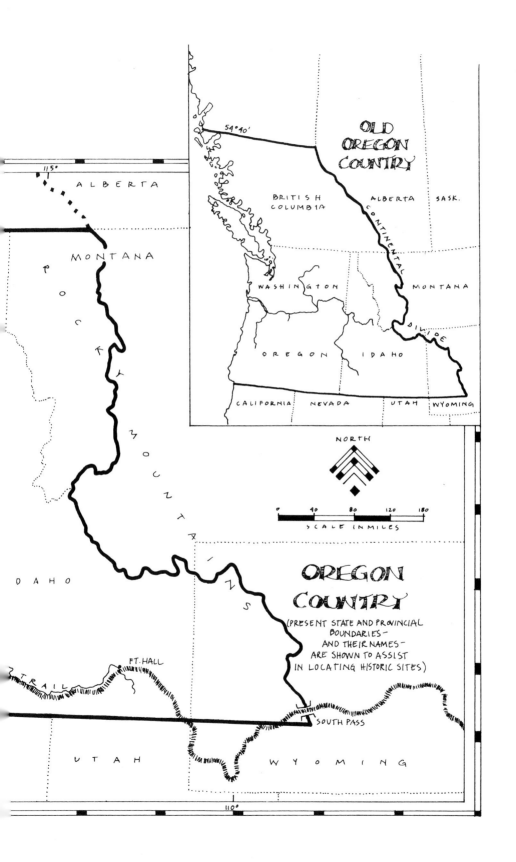

That Balance

TERENCE

OREGON HISTORICAL

So Rare
THE STORY OF OREGON

O'DONNELL

SOCIETY PRESS

COVER: Hand-tinted lantern slides from the Oregon Historical Society Photographic Archives' Frank Branch Riley Collection. Riley was an early and vociferous booster of Oregon. In the 1910s, he began touring the country with the lecture "The Lure of the Great Northwest," which he illustrated with these specially made lantern slides. *Front cover:* Lost Lake with Mount Hood in the background, OrHi 96392; Multnomah Falls, OrHi 96396; Crown Point overlooking the Columbia River Gorge, OrHi 96399. *Back cover:* St. Johns Bridge over the Willamette River, OrHi 96393; Loggers and felled tree, OrHi 96397; Dipnetting at Celilo Falls, Benjamin Gifford photograph, OrHi 96397.

TITLE PAGE: Physical profile of northern portion of Oregon. Cross-section runs west-east from Pacific Ocean and Coast Range to Mount Hood, across high desert and Wallowas, ending at Snake River Canyon at Oregon-Idaho border. Vertical height exaggeration is ten times.

Library of Congress Cataloging-in-Publications Data

O'Donnell, Terence.
    That balance so rare.

    Bibliography: p.
    Includes index.
    1. Oregon—History. 2. Oregon—History—Chronology.
I. Title
    F876.033 1988   979.5   88-28949
    ISBN 0-87595-202-x

The paper used in this publication meets the minimum requirements of American National Standard for Information Sciences—Permanence of Paper for Printed Library Materials. ANSI Z39.48-1984. ∞

This volume was designed and produced by the Oregon Historical Society Press.

Printed in the United States of America.

To Thomas Vaughan
with gratitude

Contents

1
Figures in the Dawn

The great cataclysmic events were over: exploding mountains, lava floods, draining seas, the massive, dragging glaciers—all this cosmic tumult, breaking up the land and reforming it eon after eon, had finally spent itself. Rivers, rain, wind, and pounding surf continued to age the earth's face, but in general, what we now call Oregon is what finally came to rest ten thousand years ago.

Then, as now, the Pacific drove in to crash against the high-cliffed coast while ocean clouds drifted east to drench with rain the seaward slopes of what we have come to call the Coast Range. Beyond the mountains, the long valley lay with its meander of river—though here there is a difference between then and now: it is believed before humans came, the valley floor was forest rather than the present open plain. To the east, however, the land lay much as we see it today: the Cascades soaring up to the arid lava plains of the high country—rim rock and deep canyons to the northeast, the southwest dense with mountain peaks. From the estuaries and rain forests of the coast to the valley—lush and almost tropical—to the interior with its distances and skies and tingling, sage-scented air, it was a landscape of ravishing variety, as it is today.

There is one respect, however, in which it was a profoundly different place from now—it was silent. The only sounds were the sounds of the place itself: falling rain; the singing rush of rivers; an avalanche's crash; the boom and hiss of surf; fire, and its roar and crackle in a forest tindered by a

[*continued on page* 4]   1

Petroglyphs, designs scratched or carved into rock, are difficult to date but certainly the Indians executed them before the coming of the whites. The bluffs above the Columbia River were favored sites, but many of the petroglyphs have been lost due to dam building. (OHS neg. Loring Roll 23, frame 4A-5)

The Fort Rock sandal was discovered by Dr. Luther
Cressman during excavations in Lake County during
the 1930s. It is made of sagebrush and according to
carbon dating, is about ten thousand years old.
(Photo courtesy L. S. Cressman. OHS neg. OrHi
80007)

lightning strike; wind, screaming through the gulleys, creaking the giant oaks, whispering the prairie grass—and bird song, thunder, and the cries of animals.

This was the world into which one day about ten thousand years ago human beings stepped: Asiatics from what is now Siberia. Why they left we do not know—famine, drought, more likely hunters following their prey. In any event, they crossed by an Alaskan land bridge—and probably by boat as well—to North America. Settlement appears to have first occurred in the interior, later along the Columbia River, and finally on the coast.

The natives of the coast lived in small villages of plank houses, strung along the banks of the streams that poured down from the coastal mountains into the Pacific. These streams, as well as a vegetation tropical in its impenetrability, isolated the coastal tribes, and thus a diversity of languages developed. All, however, lived from the land and the sea, berries and game, salmon and shellfish. To the people of the Columbia and lower Willamette (the most populous of these first Oregonians), salmon was of greater importance and used for trade as well as sustenance. For the tribes of the inland valleys, however, nuts and roots and game took salmon's place. A pleasing and literally fragrant aspect of the culture of these three peoples was their use of cedar for almost all of their material needs—clothing, shelter, utensils, containers, and, of course, their superb canoes.

South, in the vicinity of the present Klamath lakes, the native people were marsh and lakeside dwellers, subsisting on plants and waterfowl and living in semi-subterranean, earth-domed lodges. Their neighbors to the east, in what is now called the Great Basin, also subsisted on waterfowl and plants—when they could be found, for the natives of the Great Basin often faced near starvation—but these people were few in number, mainly nomadic, and lived in little bell-shaped huts made of willow whips.

Finally, there were the plateau tribes of northeastern Oregon. Horseborne by about the eighteenth century, they were a vigorous people and wide-ranging, from the barren steppes of the upper Columbia to the high alpine valleys of the Wallowas, living, when settled, in long, tepee-type mat houses.

Such, then, were the first Oregonians. By the time of their contact with whites in the early nineteenth century, they numbered tens of thousands, these divided into nearly one hundred bands and tribes. Though a people of

4

many differences, in physique and language for example, they did to some degree share a common culture. Most were animists, believing all things, whether rock or tree, stream or star, animal or man, were imbued with spirit. Thus, for them, all the world was living. And with this living world they in turn lived in close communion. Weather, animals, the earth, its fruits—they mingled with these things, becoming one with them: the flesh and skin of animals; the berries, bulbs, and nuts of earth; the cleansing water; the shade of trees; the warmth of fire. There were no separate orders: man, animals, matter. All were one.

Many of them held, too, that the creator of this world was the coyote god, *Spilyay*. Spilyay, in whose belly lived his three wise sisters in the form of huckleberries, is clever, capricious, lascivious, mischievous, and endlessly inventive—surely one of the most human and entertaining gods mankind has created.

Spilyay, as well as many other figures, animal and human, is the subject of a large body of folk tales. Fortunately, a number of these were translated from their oral sources and published. Most of the tales tell how Oregon began, how the ocean, the rivers and the lakes, the mountains and the valleys, the prairies and the deserts came to be—in the process giving us an unequaled sense of our natural world. If Oregon has a true folk literature in the sense of being distinct to the region and worthy of esteem, it is this rich gift to us from those who came here first.

2

Landfalls & Forest Trails

It probably happened somewhere on the southern coast. Exactly when is difficult to say—four to five hundred years ago. Perhaps one day a woman, straightening up from tearing mussels from the rock, gazed out across "the river with one bank," as the natives called the ocean, to see it first: the great black-bodied bird with its strangely configured wings riding the swells, its beak, pole thin, jutting up at an angle from the head. As the years passed, the people were to see more and more of these great black-bodied birds. One wonders if they knew, for them at least, these were birds of ill omen that would one day bring their doom.

It began with a myth. According to the myth, there was a passage or strait on the north coast of North America that connected the Atlantic and Pacific oceans, that long-sought-for advantage, a direct sea route from Western Europe to Asia. Around this central myth clustered others. "Marine lying reached the climax and borders on the heroic," wrote the historian Hubert Howe Bancroft. For example, somewhere on the Oregon coast there flourished the kingdom of Fu Sang, founded by a Buddhist monk and his disciples from Afghanistan. Here they created a great civilization centered on the Fu Sang tree and its magic powers!

It was the desire to see and plunder such marvelous places, but in particular to find that passage to the East, that accounts for the presence off the Oregon coast in the sixteenth century and thereafter of the great black-bodied birds—the ships of the explorers.

[*continued on page* 10]   7

FRANCISCVS, DRAKE.

De. Larmessin, sculp.

Sir Francis Drake, England's "merry" buccaneer, is
thought to have reached the southern Oregon coast in
1579. (OHS neg. OrHi 52890)

Robert Gray's initial voyage to the Pacific in 1787-88 was the occasion of the first American landing on the Northwest coast. But it was an event darkened by tragedy. Indians pursued Gray's black cabin boy, Markus Lopius, and according to the ship's second mate, "drenched their knives and speers with savage feury in the boddy of the unfortunate youth." Gray, in his anger, named the moorage Murderer's Bay. It is now called Tillamook Bay. (OHS negs. OrHi 26699 and OrHi 984)

So far as one can determine, the first of these was a Spanish expedition sailing from Navidad, Mexico, in 1542 under the command of Juan Rodríguez Cabrillo. Following many mishaps—including the death of Cabrillo—his pilot, Bartolomé Ferrelo, reached the vicinity of the Rogue River in the spring of 1543. Torrential storms prohibited a landing and indeed were so severe the crew was assembled to take their death vows. Perhaps this was the first of the great black-bodied birds the natives on the shore observed with bafflement and fear.

A few years later, Spain's great enemy, that "merry, careful" buccaneer Sir Francis Drake, was also anchored off the southern Oregon coast before being driven south by storms. He was searching in the *Golden Hind* for the Northwest Passage—as well as Spanish treasure ships to plunder.

It was another Spaniard, however, Martín de Aguilar, thought to have been off present Port Orford, who gives us our first description of the Oregon coast, a "rapid and abundant river, with ash trees, willows and brambles and other trees of Castile on its banks." But he, too, for reasons of weather and currents, was unable to land.

At this same time, the galleon trade between Spain's new possessions in the Philippines and Mexico began. The course of these ships was south of the Oregon latitudes, but occasionally, some were blown off course. One of those, the *San Francisco Xavier*, wrecked at the base of Neahkahnie Mountain in 1707, leaving behind a cargo of beeswax, remnants of which may still be found on the nearby beaches.

It was in the last quarter of the eighteenth century, however, that exploration began in earnest; navigators searching now not only for the Northwest Passage but also for "the great river of the West," sometimes called the "Oregon," now known, of course, as the Columbia. In August of 1775, the distinguished Spanish explorer Bruno de Hezeta located the mouth of the river, but his crew was so weakened by scurvy they were unable to man the sails and cross the bar. Regretfully, Hezeta was forced to sail away. Two years later, an even greater mariner, English captain James Cook, searching for the river, passed it unknowingly on a stormy night. He was followed in 1778 by his countryman, John Meares, who deemed it no river at all and so named its estuary Deception Bay and its northern promontory Cape Disappointment.

10

Captain George Vancouver, commissioned by the British Admiralty to make an official survey of the Northwest Coast, passed the mouth of the river in the spring of 1792. He, too, denied the river's existence despite the evidence: gulls, earthen-colored water, drifting logs, and cross-currents. "Not considering the opening worthy of more attention I continued our pursuit to the N.W.," wrote the great explorer Vancouver.

At fault was Vancouver's skepticism. He believed the great river and the Northwest Passage to be no more than sailors' yarns, thus finding it particularly appropriate he sailed from England in search of both on April Fool's Day. However, if Vancouver failed to find the Columbia, he did prove later the Northwest Passage did not, after all, exist.

But the Columbia again and again resisted discovery. How at last it was discovered is a roundabout tale indeed. As with merchants elsewhere, the merchants of Boston were anxious to trade with the Chinese but were prevented by the fact they produced little the Chinese wanted. By now, however, these merchants had heard of the great profits made by irregular traders, Russian and British, selling Northwest furs to the Orient. Why not join them in the pickings? Thus was born the Pacific triangular trade. In October of 1787, Captains John Kendrick and Robert Gray were sent out by their backers from Boston with a cargo of buttons and beads, blue cloth, and bits of iron and copper. Arriving on the Oregon coast ten months later, they bargained with the natives for sea otter pelts, sold them in the Orient, bought tea and perhaps some silk and spices, after which Gray set sail for Boston, the first American sailor to circumnavigate the globe.

Gray's name, however, would be relatively unknown had it not been for his second voyage to the Oregon coast and a certain decision he made at eight o'clock on the morning of 11 May 1792.

A few weeks before this day so crucial to American expansion, Gray, as with Vancouver, was off the Oregon coast. As did Vancouver, he, too, noted at latitude 46° 53' a great flow of muddy water fanning from the shore. Passing on to the strait of Juan de Fuca, Gray encountered Vancouver and informed him of his belief these muddy waters might well signify the mouth of the Great River of the West. The eminent navigator was not about to entertain such notions from this unknown American trader. No "reason to alter our ópinions," wrote Vancouver.

[*continued on page* 16]   11

Close friends while serving together in the army, William Clark was persuaded by Meriwether Lewis to join the expedition to the Pacific as co-leader. The two men in their differing characters—Clark the more forceful, Lewis the gentler—complemented each other to good effect. On his return, Clark devoted the rest of his life to Indian affairs. (OHS neg. OrHi 13082)

Meriwether Lewis, an army officer, served as Jefferson's secretary and then was appointed by the latter to lead the expedition to the Pacific. Of a poetic temperament and a lover of plants and animals, Lewis recorded the expedition with distinction. On his return, he was appointed governor of the Louisiana Territory. He died at the age of thirty-five in a country inn. Whether a suicide or murder, it was never determined. (OHS neg. OrHi 4582)

In 1955, the Oregon Historical Society built a replica
of Lewis and Clark's Fort Clatsop on the site of the
original fort. The design was based upon the floor
plan sketched by Captain Clark on the elkhide cover
of his fieldbook. The fort is fifty feet square, with a
parade ground in the center and quarters for officers
and men to either side. In 1958, the fort was designated
a national memorial. (Dean W. Bond photo. OHS neg.
OrHi 81790)

President Thomas Jefferson was particularly concerned that Lewis and Clark keep journals "with great pains and accuracy." He further insisted they make copies "on the paper of birch as less liable to injury from damp than common paper." Though a narrative based on the journals was published in 1814, the journals themselves lay untouched, and largely unknown, for seventy-five years in the vaults of the

American Philosophical Society. In 1904, a century after they were written, these most important documents of American exploration were finally published. Here, drawings from Clark's journals depict Clatsop Indians and a white salmon trout. (From R.G. Thwaites' *Original Journals of the Lewis and Clark Expedition, 1804-06*, v.IV, New York: 1905. OHS negs. OrHi 81800 & 81801)

15

But Gray was not about to alter his opinions, either, and started out to confirm his belief and find his river.

At four in the morning on 11 May Gray arrived at the river's mouth. Then, even more than now, the Columbia bar was one of the most treacherous on earth. They waited, four hours they waited, until there came that right convergence of currents, tide, and wind. Gray gave the command, and the prow of his ship, the *Columbia Rediviva*, its figurehead holding before it the escutcheon of the American republic, crashed through the breakers into the waters of the Great River of the West, which from then on would be known as the Columbia.

Robert Gray's discovery did much to encourage other American fur traders who used the Columbia as a winter haven and who, by the end of the century, controlled the sea otter trade. Of more universal significance is that this rather offhand happenstance of discovery was, outside of arctic regions, among the last major coastal geographical features of the world to be revealed. But more immediate and long lasting in its consequences was that, with Gray and his discovery, the presence of the United States was established for the first time in western America as well as on the Pacific— a presence on which the United States would later base its claim to possession.

Gray, after a week or so of trading with the Indians, left without investigating the interior into which the river led. This was done several months later by Lieutenant William Broughton who, as Vancouver's second in command, had arrived to verify Gray's discovery. Broughton spent three weeks on the river, proceeding as far as the mouth of the Columbia Gorge. The log of this voyage provides us with our first real description of the Oregon Country. It was, Broughton wrote, "the most beautiful landscape that can be imagined." He went on to describe the wooded islands and water meadows; the sand spits, bluffs, and beaches; the river banks thick with wild lavender and mint; the groves of alder, maple, birch, willow, poplar, oak, and long slopes of fir. He remarked as well on the wildlife: flights of duck and geese, brown cranes, white swans, otter, beaver, deer, and elk. Finally, there were the mountains in their perfect white repose, supreme above it all.

Broughton, as with the Americans before him, was quite taken by the natives. John Boit, of Gray's crew, had written, "The Men at Columbia's

River are STRAIT LIMB'D, fine looking fellows, and the women are very pretty." Broughton found they surpassed other tribes in their "paints of different colors, feathers and other ornaments," and in all instances, they were civil and often helpful. One old chief was so much so Broughton named the stretch of river that passed his village (in the vicinity of present Vancouver) "Friendly Reach."

There was, however, one disquieting feature in this Edenic scene. All up and down the river, on bluff and sandspit, and trestled high beyond the reach of animals, stood the funerary canoes that held the bodies of the dead. With their black prows silhouetted somberly against the sky, they were a kind of prefigurement of what was to come—the disease, killing, and heartsickness that would go on for a century and end by almost obliterating the native peoples from the face of their lovely earth.

Such, then, was the penetration of Oregon from the sea. The next would be by land. The idea had originated with the American Philosophical Society, and to promote it, Thomas Jefferson and Alexander Hamilton had contributed $12.50 each. It was Jefferson, however, who followed through, persuading Congress to fund an expedition across the continent to the Northwest Coast. He chose his secretary, Meriwether Lewis, to head the expedition. Lewis, in turn, chose William Clark, an army comrade, to share the command. Their purposes were three: to determine a route between the Missouri and Columbia rivers and thereby facilitate travel and trade; to report on the flora, fauna, and geography of the region; and to establish friendly relations with the Indians. Another purpose, though not stated, was to lay further basis for new territorial claims on the region should the United States decide to make them.

The expedition departed from St. Louis in the spring of 1804. It proceeded upstream in a leisurely fashion though not without incident, for there were desertions and thievery, all severely punished with the lash. Upon arriving at the Platte River, they had reached the end of their world: "We were now about to penetrate," wrote Lewis, "a country at least 2,000 miles in width, on which the foot of civilized man has never trodden; the good or evil it had in store for us was for experiment yet to determine."

More good than evil was their lot on the westward trek. Despite the cold, they wintered comfortably near present Bismarck, North Dakota. What difficulties they suffered were minor, as for example the behavior of the

Indians they encountered after crossing the Great Divide. "We were caressed and besmeared with their grease and paint till I was heartily tired of the national hug," wrote Lewis. Also, they grew weary of a diet consisting of so much fish, but this they remedied upon reaching the Columbia by purchasing forty dogs.

On 15 November 1805, nineteen months after their departure from St. Louis, the expedition saw the Pacific Ocean at the mouth of the Columbia. Here they spent a miserable winter in a little log stockade (Fort Clatsop) they built on a low hill above a bog of tidal creeks. It rained every day but six. They spent these dreary days making salt at what is today Seaside, hunting game which was scarce, and fighting the abundant fleas. On Christmas they celebrated with "pore Elk, so much Spoiled that we eate it thro mear necessity, Some Spoiled Pounded fish and a fiew roots."

There was also much sickness: colds, dysentery, and rheumatism. Many of the men acquired venereal diseases from the natives who, in turn, had been infected by the sailors of the fur trade. The natives had less resistance to disease than whites and thus more often died when struck by these sicknesses. Indeed, in the scant thirteen years since Gray and Broughton, there had been a shocking deterioration in the natives, far fewer of the "fine looking fellows" and "women very pretty" Gray's party had noted. And instead of the "deer and otter skin" garments reported by Broughton, many now wore the tattered castoffs of the foreign sailors. One native woman wore a more permanent adornment: the name "J. Bowman" tattooed on her arm.

With spring the expedition was only too happy to be on its way, departing the Columbia in March of 1806, arriving in St. Louis in September, thus completing one of the most remarkable journeys of exploration in the history of the Americas and establishing another basis for United States claims in the West. Of more immediate importance was the fact Lewis and Clark's reports now made known to all that here was a place suitable for settlement.

3
Beavers & Bibles

In the winter of 1784, a German immigrant named John Jacob Astor arrived in Baltimore, Maryland. He began his American business enterprise by selling seven flutes at a profit and thence went on to more and greater profits—though through the sale of furs, not flutes. By 1810, and now a magnate in the trade, Astor decided to establish his new subsidiary, the Pacific Fur Company, at the mouth of the Columbia River. His scheme was to sell goods to the Indians and the Russians in Alaska, and in return buy furs from them to sell in the Orient. It could not have been a more promising scheme. In operation, it hardly could have been more disastrous.

One contingent of the staff Astor sent to the Columbia traveled by land, the other by sea, the latter in the *Tonquin* captained by Jonathan Thorn. Captain Thorn turned out to be a psychopath, and through his madness, eight men were lost at sea before the *Tonquin* reached its destination. This destination lay on the south side of the Columbia's mouth, a rise of land at the end of a little bay at present Astoria.

At first glance, it seemed most inviting. "The weather was magnificent," wrote Gabriel Franchère, one of the company clerks, "and all Nature smiled. The forest looked like pleasant groves and the leaves like flowers." The trees in this forest, however, often had a girth of fifty feet, grew densely together, and were interspersed by giant boulders. Few of the company clerks had ever felled a tree and none under such conditions. After planting the twelve

[*continued on page* 22]   19

Astoria in 1841. Following the sale of Astoria to the British North West Company in 1813, Astoria was renamed Fort George and continued to be so known until the boundary decision of 1846 when the original name was restored. Astoria is the oldest American settlement in the West. (From Charles Wilkes' *Narrative of the United States Exploring Expedition*, Philadelphia, 1845. OHS neg. OrHi 702)

John Jacob Astor, founder of Astoria, the first American settlement in the West. (OHS neg. OrHi 54)

McLoughlin had three principal duties at the fort. The first was to make money: to trap out the whole of the Northwest, bring in the pelts, dress them, and send them off to London. He did, and the company profited handsomely.

A second duty was to control the natives. He did this by prohibiting certain earlier practices. For example, it had been common practice to offer rum to the natives and then—after they were all addicted—to trade with them, a little rum for many furs. Also, McLoughlin always kept his word, whether for reward or punishment—always. In return for all these things the natives named their children after him, made him a chief, "White-Headed Eagle," and, it is said, carved his face, this white man's face, into their totem poles.

McLoughlin's third duty was a vexing one. He was to prevent settlement in the Oregon Country for the following reasons. By now, the region was claimed by both the United States and Britain by right of discovery—Britain basing its claim on Broughton's voyage up the Columbia River. Since these claims could not be reconciled, the two countries concluded a treaty in 1818 that provided that the region be open to the citizens of both countries until 1828, when once again the problem would be discussed.

Such was the treaty, but McLoughlin's instructions were to discourage the American presence in any way possible. For one thing, there was the truth of the old adage, where the ax of the settler rang, the trapper must certainly disappear, and trapping and the selling of furs was, after all, the company's business. Also, it was obvious if the American ssettled in any number, American claims to the region would be strengthened.

By seeing to it that the area south of the Columbia would be thoroughly trapped out, McLoughlin did succeed in discouraging the encroachments of American trappers, but in forestalling settlement he failed. In a sense this failure began within, for the fort itself was a settlement in several respects. In the year of its establishment, grain was sown, orchards planted, and cattle allowed to multiply, resulting in a farm of fifteen hundred acres. Then there was the population of the fort, no camp at a crossing of forest paths but a community of several hundred with schools, churches, and other attributes of permanence.

More fundamental than this was an act of McLoughlin's compassion.

Upon retirement, the company's French Canadian trappers were required by their contracts to return to Quebec for mustering out. Beginning in 1829, McLoughlin permitted them to take land and farm on the banks of the Willamette near present St. Paul. Thus did settlement begin in Oregon—and with French Canadian trappers, not American pioneers, a fact sometimes forgotten.

The Americans, however, were coming, though through a circumstance that initially had no connection with Oregon whatsoever. In the years 1824-36, there occurred in the eastern United States a born-again, evangelical movement that placed great emphasis on missionary work. In 1831, four Oregon Country Indians journeyed to St. Louis seeking knowledge, it is said, of Christianity. Thus was kindled that fire of evangelicalism that would bring, in numbers, the first Americans to Oregon. "Let two suitable men, unencumbered with families, and possessing the spirit of martyrs throw themselves into the nation [the natives of Oregon]. Live with them—learn their language—preach Christ to them and, as the way opens, introduce schools, agriculture, and the arts of civilized life." So proclaimed the great Methodist divine, Wilbur Fisk, in 1833.

His call was answered the following year by a thirty-one-year-old Methodist, Jason Lee, a dedicated evangelist ready to suffer all hardships to save the natives of Oregon from damnation. Two years later in 1836, four missionaries—Marcus and Narcissa Whitman and Henry and Eliza Spalding, sponsored by the Congregational, Presbyterian, and Dutch Reformed churches—departed for the Oregon Country, like Lee, with trapping parties. Both groups were treated kindly by Dr. McLoughlin and given sound advice on where best to establish their respective missions. Lee and his associates settled near Salem while the Whitmans and Spaldings began their work in the vicinity of today's Walla Walla, Washington, and Lewiston, Idaho. Over the next decade, these mission stations not only gained in population due to periodic reinforcements from the East, they also created substations: the Methodists at the Dalles on the Columbia, Oregon City, and Clatsop Plains; and the Whitman-Spalding group at Spokane. In other words, by the early 1840s, the American missionaries had established seven settlements in the Oregon Country.

This major contribution to the settlement of Oregon by the American

[*continued on page* 30]

Inspector General
Mansfield's sketch of
Fort Vancouver, 1854.
(OHS neg. OrHi 81948)

Fort Vancouver. (From
Charles Wilkes' *Life in
Oregon Country Before the
Emigration*, Ashland,
Oregon: The Oregon
Book Society, 1974-75.
OHS neg. OrHi 81796)

28

Francis Norbert Blanchet arrived at Fort Vancouver in 1838, the first Roman Catholic priest to reside in the Oregon Country. Later, he was appointed archbishop of the diocese of Oregon, the second oldest diocese in the United States. Blanchet served as the shepherd of his flock for more than forty years. According to his contemporary, Judge Matthew Deady, and in the words of the Deady authority, Malcolm Clark, the archbishop "combined the wisdom of the serpent with the harmlessness of the dove." (OHS neg. OrHi 1713)

The early development of the Oregon Country was largely due to a fashion—the fashion for beaver hats. And it was an enormous trade. Between 1834-37, for example, nearly half a million skins were handled by the Hudson's Bay Company at Fort Vancouver. By the middle of the 1840s, however, the beaver were trapped out and the fashion passed. (OHS neg. OrHi 82159)

29

missionaries is beyond dispute. Their success in Christianizing and civilizing the natives of Oregon is another matter, a tale of basically good intentions frustrated at every turn.

In the first place, the missionaries were distracted by their own internal difficulties: frequent squabbling among themselves, little understanding from their distant headquarters in the East, and finally, the necessity of devoting much of their time to providing for their own needs, thus leaving little energy for the instruction of the natives.

It was, however, their problems with the natives themselves that were insurmountable. Many of the latter were to some degree migratory, so sustained instruction at the mission sites was often difficult. Far more distressing was the fact the missionaries were obliged to love a people whose habits they abhorred—gambling, drinking, stealing, irregular sexual conduct, the near nakedness, and an almost total indifference to cleanliness, bodily or otherwise. Worse, the missionaries were signally unsuccessful in convincing the Indians that in practicing these habits they were sinning.

If the missionaries had problems with the natives, so, too, did the natives have problems with the missionaries. In the beginning, the missionaries were a novelty, but the novelty rather soon wore off. In the beginning, also, the missionaries had distributed material rewards, but these soon dwindled, provoking one Cayuse to complain "God is stingy." Baptism, as far as the natives could see, had not improved their prowess in the hunt, in war, or in love. The missionaries' continued descriptions of the torments of hell both puzzled and depressed them. Soon, too, doubts developed as to the divine origins of the missionaries' message. "Where are these laws from?" asked a Walla Walla chief. "Are they from God or from the earth? . . . I think they are from the earth, because, from what I know of white men, they do not honor these laws." Finally, the natives had reason to question one of Christianity's cardinal tenets. In 1838, two Roman Catholic priests, Fathers Francis Norbert Blanchet and Modeste Demers, arrived in the Oregon Country evangelizing in competition with the Protestants. But the fierce antagonism that flared between the two religious bodies did not deter the missionaries from haranguing the confused natives on the supreme importance of brotherly love.

It took no more than a decade for the Protestant missionary effort to founder. In 1844, Jason Lee was removed from his post. The following year, the *Methodist Annual Report* confessed, "The hopes of the mission for the future depend primarily upon the success of the Gospel among the immigrants." As for the Whitmans and the Spaldings, in November 1847, the Cayuse, convinced Dr. Whitman was purposely infecting them with smallpox, slaughtered him, his wife, and twelve of their associates. (Dr. Whitman had in fact poisoned the natives' dogs and also injected his melons with an emetic to discourage thievery.)

Though failing in their mission to Christianize and civilize the native Oregonians, the missionaries nonetheless had a profound effect. For one thing, they established schools that became colleges, such as Willamette, Pacific, Linfield, and Lewis and Clark (formerly Albany College), that continue after nearly a century and a half to enrich the state. Also, by reason of their letters and reports concerning the virtues of the Oregon Country, they encouraged immigration. Finally, they planted the seed in 1838 that would bear the fruit of statehood in 1859. This was a memorial Lee carried to Washington, D.C., asking Congress to establish its jurisdiction over the Oregon Country. "We flatter ourselves we are the germe of a great State."

4

Eden Seekers

The immigration encouraged by the missionaries began in the early 1840s, for a number of reasons. The Mississippi, Missouri, and Ohio river valleys from which so many pioneers started out were in the most economically depressed region of the country. This, combined with the promise of free land in the West, was a weighty incentive. Also, no region in the country was more unhealthy than these valleys—malaria endemic and a scourge—whereas Oregon already had its reputation of being a tonic place. Finally, there was plain American restlessness.

As there were different reasons for the immigration, so there were different kinds of immigrants. There were the enterprising, but there were also the failures and the lawless. Also, there was one large body of pioneers, nearly half, who in many cases set out with much reluctance—the women. On the whole, however, the wagon train pioneers were a fairly homogeneous body. Except for the bachelor drovers and household hands, most were families. Almost all were Protestants. Few were people of means and few impoverished, since it took money to buy the gear to get to Oregon. Finally, the majority were farmers.

A distinction is sometimes made between the kinds of people who went to Oregon and those who favored California. Some say the distinction is valid. From the beginning, California tended to attract the single adventurer, particularly with the advent of the gold rush. Oregon, on the other hand, often attracted sober and respectable individuals. Hall J. Kelley, the Boston

33

schoolteacher who first encouraged immigration to Oregon, called for "pious and educated young men," and, as we have seen, the first American settlers in Oregon were in fact missionaries. Also, that memorial Lee carried to Congress in 1838 made it clear the settlers did not care to be joined by the "reckless adventurer," by the "renegade of civilization," or by the "unprincipled sharpers of Spanish America," the Californians. Some of the diaries and letters of the immigrants confirm this attitude. Charles Pitman, traveling with a group bound for California that had begun to have second thoughts, wrote, "If things are not as anticipated when we left, in fact the Aristocracy or respectable portion of the companies will go to this valley." And Jesse Applegate wrote to his brother, "almost all the respectable portion of the California immigrants are going on the new road to Oregon—and nearly all the respectable immigrants that went last year to California came this year to Oregon." It is all marvelously summed up in the apocryphal story of a branch in the Oregon Trail, the route south to California marked by a cairn of gold quartz, the one north by a sign lettered "To Oregon." Those who could read came to Oregon.

The trek started in the spring at Independence, Missouri, that "great Babel upon the border of the wilderness." Here, the wagons—on average ten feet long with two-foot sides—were stocked with tools, clothes, seed, perhaps a harmonium, a clock; and the staples: bacon, beans, sugar, salt, coffee, and probably a keg of whiskey. They had two thousand miles to go, and it would take about six months.

Before starting out, or shortly thereafter, captains were chosen, and because they were entering a land where no civil authority existed, it was necessary to draw up regulations covering all aspects of behavior. "No profane swearing, no obscene conversation, or immoral conduct, allowed in this company." There was also the thorny problem of whether to travel on the Sabbath.

The first four-fifths of the journey was ordinarily not a hardship, at least for the men who, relieved of the routine of farm chores, often found it a lark. It was decidedly less so for the women because it was hard to keep house and manage children in a jolting ten-foot box, and there were almost always clouds of asphyxiating dust kicked up by the vanguard. Then there were the campsites. Though these could be in a pleasant grove of trees, they were usually well back from the river bottoms to avoid dampness and mosquitoes. This meant for the women long distances to haul water. Then, too, the campsites often had been occupied the night before by a forward party and so could be rankly odoriferous with animal and human feces.

There were other problems as well: shortages of grass for the cattle, raging rivers to cross, sometimes bitter hand-to-hand fighting between men. Death by drowning and by the accidental discharge of firearms was not uncommon and killed more of the immigrants than the natives. Indeed, it is estimated that between 1840-60 more natives were slaughtered by immigrants than vice versa.

But there were pleasures, too. Despite the fights, there was considerable camaraderie. "This trip finds us together like a band of brothers." Many of the women might have said the same. At night there were prayer meetings to attend or a fiddle to dance to or friends with whom to share a jug. And as seventeen-year-old Susan Parish wrote, "Where there are young people together there is always lovemaking."

On the last leg of the journey, however—from Fort Hall in Idaho to Oregon's Willamette Valley—the pleasures were few indeed. Now food supplies were low, both immigrants and animals exhausted by the long months of the trek. Worst of all, there lay before them the dreaded Blue Mountains which, because of the steepness of the grades, could be crossed only with the aid of block and tackle. The immigrants prayed that now, in late September, snow would not come early to the mountains.

Upon reaching the Willamette Valley and the other major valleys of western Oregon, the immigrants—fifty-three thousand of them between 1840 and 1860—without exception were glad the journey was over.

And what did they find? The geography of the Willamette Valley was the same then as now: roughly one hundred miles long, twenty to thirty miles wide, flat green prairie swelling here and there into buttes, oak savannas, streams pouring from the two mountain ranges through slopes of hemlock, spruce, fir, and incense cedar to feed the river that meandered the whole of the Valley's length and gave the place its name. What astonished the immigrants, however, was not so much the Valley, about as Edenic as they had expected, but something above it—that great white escarpment against the blue of the eastern sky—the mountains.

[*continued on page* 38]

"Distance was the enemy, not Indians or crossings or weather or thirst or plains or mountains, but distance, the empty awesome face of distance. . . . There was no end to it. . . . Morning and night it was there unchanged, hill and cloud and skyline beyond reach or understanding." From *The Way West*, A. B. Guthrie, W. Sloane Associates, 1949. (Oregon Department of Transportation photo. OHS neg. CN 006109)

When sketched by Henry Warre in 1845, Oregon City had a population of about five hundred. Here, at the Main Street House, one could get a good meal of potatoes, boiled salmon, coffee, and for dessert, bread sopped in Hawaiian molasses. The hotel was head-quarters for the town's literary society as well as for the members of the provisional legislature. Of the latter, the secretary of the literary society wrote that they had at the end of their session, "the appearance of having just been caught robbing a turkey roost." (OHS neg. OrHi 791)

With the boundary decision of 1846, Dr. John McLoughlin retired from the Hudson's Bay Company to live in Oregon City, the town he founded in 1842 and where he later became an American citizen. However, the last years of the "Father of Oregon" were embittered ones. "I planted all I had here and the government has confiscated my property," he charged after the United States Congress refused to recognize his land claim, an injustice not rectified until after his death. (OHS neg. OrHi 248)

There were other surprises, too, some pleasant, some not. By the mid-1840s the Valley was pretty well hunted out, so game was scarce. Also, the immigrants were disappointed that the wild plum of their native forests did not grow in their new home. More disappointing yet, there were no bee trees filled with honey. On the other hand, hazel nuts abounded as did a variety of berries. The climate, too, was welcome: the temperate winters, the gentle summers, the relative absence of thunder and lightning, and a novelty and delight to all—the rainbows.

This, then, was the world where the immigrants settled. Most typically, or anyway most ideally, they claimed land—the expected 640 acres for a man and wife—on the prairie margins, close to both timber and open land. They needed timber to build their houses and barns, open land for their animals to graze on and to plant wheat—shelter and food, the bases of their life.

But these things could take time, and the beginnings were difficult. For instance, due to the absence of wool, cotton, and flax, there was a great shortage of cloth. Provisions were usually adequate for the old settlers but were badly taxed by the sudden yearly increases in population brought on by the migrations. Peter Burnett, an immigrant of 1843 and first governor of California, provides us with a picture.

At every public meeting, it was easy to distinguish the new from the old settlers. They were lank, lean, hungry and tough. We were ruddy, ragged and rough. They were dressed in broadcloth, wore linen-bosomed shirts and black cravats while we wore very coarse patched clothes; the art of patching was understood to perfection in Oregon. But while they dressed better than we did, we fed better than they. They wanted our provisions while we wanted their material for clothing.

Many of the men immigrants were childish, most of them discouraged, and all of them more or less embarrassed. There was necessarily, under the circumstances, a great hurry to select claims; and the newcomers had to travel over the country in the rainy season in search of homes. Their animals being poor, they found it difficult to get along as fast as they desired. There were no hotels in the country . . . the old settlers had necessarily to open their doors to the new immigrants . . . our families were often overworked in waiting upon others and our provisions vanished before the keen appetites of our new guests. They bred famine wherever they went.

No single person aided the immigrants more than did John McLoughlin. Touched by the hardships they had endured, he helped them again and again with money, supplies, and good counsel even though his instructions were to discourage settlement. But finally, the instructions were adamant: he was to discontinue all assistance. "Gentlemen," it is said he replied, "if such is your order I will serve you no longer." And he did not. McLoughlin resigned in 1846 and retired to the town he founded in 1829, the first in Oregon, indeed the first to be incorporated in the West, Oregon City.

As mentioned earlier, the wagon train immigrants were remarkably homogeneous in their makeup. The people among whom they settled were far less so. On the Tualatin Plains lived the "Rocky Mountain Boys," aging American trappers, rugged types with Indian mates and children. Across the Columbia in their library were ensconced the gentlemen of the Hudson's Bay Company with their ruby port and London journals. In the vicinity of present St. Paul, those first settlers, the French Canadians, remained on along with those two sharp thorns in the Protestant side, Fathers Blanchet and Demers. Upriver at Mission Bottom struggled the Methodists. In the towns lived yet another type—New England merchants, most of whom had arrived with their goods by ship. (This was not the only respect in which these New Englanders differed from the wagon train immigrants who, for the most part, embodied the traditions and attitudes of the southern small farmer.) Finally, there were the vanishing natives. By 1845, the Willamette Valley's two thousand settlers had outnumbered them. Such, then, was the diversity with which Oregon began.

There was, however, one common characteristic. Only seven percent of these two thousand settlers were over the age of forty-five. In other words, it was a remarkably young community and, like all young communities, boisterous. Thus, they required restraint or, that is to say, laws, particularly those relating to land title and claim jumping.

This was recognized in 1843 at Champoeg on the Willamette River. Here, about one hundred settlers met to see if they could form a provisional government, "provisional" because the boundary question had not been resolved. They succeeded, though not without considerable confusion and dissension. One of the more candid of those present, Dr. Robert Newell, wrote, "After a few days experience I became satisfied that I knew but little about the business of Legislating as the majority of my colleagues." As for

[*continued on page* 42]   39

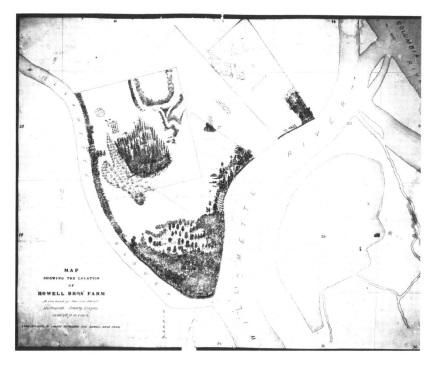

An ancient center of the Multnomah Indians and the largest fresh water island in the country, Sauvie Island takes its present name from Laurent Sauve, a Hudson's Bay employee who established a dairy farm there in 1838. American settlers came in the 1850s, with the Howell family being among the first. The dotted rectangle, upper left on the map, shows the location of the Bybee-Howell house. Restored and now maintained by the Oregon Historical Society, the house is open for viewing in the summer months. This edenic island, twenty-five minutes from Portland, is one of the country's most outstanding examples of the preservation of a rural scene near an urban area. (OHS neg. OrHi 24157)

"An immigrant will come in during the autumn," wrote a pioneer, "put himself up a log house with mud and stick chimney, split boards and shingles. His wife has few cooking utensils, few chairs. . . . You call upon him the next year and he will have a fine field ripe for the sickle. There will be a patch of corn, another of potatoes, and another of garden vegetables. His cattle and horses and hogs will be on the prairie, thriving and increasing." Depicted here is a replica of a pioneer cabin. (Georgia Pacific photo. OHS neg. OrHi 60032)

the dissension, Dr. McLoughlin and a majority of the French Canadians were understandably chary of this attempt to form a government on American lines in a region still jointly occupied by Britain and the United States. The so-called "American party" prevailed by a narrow margin.

Thus was created a body of law and a government of three branches: legislative, executive (a committee of three), and a judiciary. Despite the fact it did not have the power to tax (though when it did acquire the power it had great difficulty collecting the tax, even from its own executive committee), and despite the fact it was not officially recognized by the majority over whom it presumed to rule, the laws the new government enacted were by and large observed, though on occasion in a curious fashion. In Polk County, for example, a man was sentenced to three years imprisonment, but there being no jail and no taxes with which to build one, it was decided to sell him at auction. A local farmer bought the criminal and worked him for three years, after which he was given twenty dollars, a horse and saddle, and released.

This then, with its capital at Oregon City, was Oregon's government until 1849. As time passed, its provisions were revised. In 1845, the executive committee of three was replaced by a governor, George Abernethy, a former mission employee. Also in 1845, changes were made to allow local British participation. Still, there were stresses and strains. Some were content with the provisional nature of the government; others wanted immediate American intervention. There were also those who favored an entirely independent republic, neither American nor British. The "English party" and the "American party" were the two principal factions in these disputes. The English party consisted of the Hudson's Bay Company and the Catholic French Canadians. The American party was an uneasy alliance of the Rocky Mountain Boys, the New England merchants, the wagon train immigrants, and the Methodists. It was because of this dissension in the American party that the English party usually held the balance, at least until 1846, when the boundary question was resolved. After a generation of bickering, the British demanding everything north of the Columbia, the Americans demanding everything south of Alaska, the present boundaries were finally agreed upon by negotiation.

The 1846 treaty was not popular in Oregon. In particular, the provision permitting the Hudson's Bay Company to keep its land at Fort Vancouver—that fort where so many of the missionaries and settlers had received succor from the hands of Dr. McLoughlin—was resented. "Man is a preposterous pig; probably the greediest animal that crawls upon this planet," wrote Frances Fuller Victor, Oregon's first historian, commenting on this desire to grab Fort Vancouver, too.

5
Decade of Decisions

Following the boundary settlement, three events occurred that had a profound effect on Oregon. The first began on the morning of 8 December 1847 when George Abernethy addressed the legislature gathered in the Methodist Church by the falls at Oregon City. "Our relations with the Indians becomes every year more embarrassing," warned the governor. "They see the white man occupying their lands, rapidly filling up the country, and they put in a claim for pay. They have been told that a chief would come out from the United States and treat with them for their lands; they have been told this so often that they begin to doubt the truth of it."

That afternoon the legislators, obliged to leave their game of horse billiards (a kind of shuffleboard) because of falling snow, assembled again in the church. It was then they heard the news: the Cayuse Indians had slaughtered the Whitmans together with twelve members of their mission and were holding captive fifty-three women and children. The legislators acted immediately by moving that a volunteer army be formed with three objectives: rescue of the captives, punishment of the murderers, and prevention of a coalition of the Cayuse and other interior tribes. Thus began the Cayuse War, the first of the Oregon Indian wars, a bungle and a waste from beginning to end.

First of all, there was a shortage of both money and men. The provisional government's treasury contained $43.72, and as for volunteers, one settler

[*continued on page 48*]   45

Joe Meek, Oregon's first sheriff, as well as "minister plenipotentiary from the Republic of Oregon" as he called himself, was active in the creation of the provisional government, served as a legislator in that body, and in 1845 took Oregon's first census. His adventures, together with his considerable flamboyance, prompted Francis Fuller Victor to write his biography, *The River of the West*. Meek married three Indian women; the first was killed by the Bannocks, the second left him and returned to her tribe, and the third survived him on the Meek farm near Hillsboro. Pictured is an 1860 engraving of Meek. (OHS neg. OrHi 10126)

General Joseph Lane of Indiana, first governor of the Oregon Territory, is reported to have said when asked if he was interested in the appointment, "I'll be ready in 15 minutes." With statehood, he became Oregon's first United States senator. Lane, pictured here in 1849, gave his considerable energies to promoting education and attempting to settle Indian-white hostilities. His pro-slavery views around the time of the Civil War ended his political career in Oregon, and he retired to live as a recluse in Roseburg. (OHS neg. OrHi 1703)

remarked that when the war was over, "We will have great Patriots as we now have great chimney-corner warriors."

Next, to the considerable chagrin of the Americans, before they could get themselves together and proceed to the scene of the massacre, the Hudson's Bay Company had rescued the prisoners and delivered them to Oregon City. As was feared, some of the women had been violated. The wrath this provoked can be gauged from an editorial in the *Oregon Spectator* (Oregon City): "Let them [the Indians] be pursued with unrelenting hatred and hostility, until their lifeblood has atoned for their infamous deed; let them be hunted as beasts of prey; let their name and race be blotted from the face of the earth, and the places that once knew them, know them no more forever."

The formal campaign began with the arrival at The Dalles of the volunteers' commander, Colonel Cornelius Gilliam, veteran of the Black Hawk and Seminole wars, famed tracker of runaway slaves, Baptist preacher, and a man of whom it has been said that he "preferred the smoke of gunpowder to the smoke of peace pipes." The first casualty of this campaign occurred on the evening of his arrival and was reported by him in a letter to his wife: "One of the Garde shot a Squaw in the thy thinking that She was an Indian man. It apperes that she was acrolling along on the ground so that she get to plaice of appointment between her and some of our young men which I am very sorry to [say] such things do frequently occurs."

Colonel Gilliam's young men, in a manner most haphazard, fought their little war for the next six months, their ranks reduced by dysentery, drunkenness, and desertions, the latter particularly frequent when spring planting came around. Also, they had some difficulty finding the Indians and, when they did, some difficulty determining which were enemies, which friends. They never did succeed in apprehending, let alone identifying, Whitman's murderers. Finally, Colonel Gilliam by accident shot himself dead, which more or less ended the hostilities.

Though the casualties were not particularly high, since both sides were chronically short of gunpowder, it exacerbated those already difficult relations between Americans and British, Protestants and Catholics, and, most seriously, Indians and whites. The only blessing in disguise lay in the fact Oregon at last gained some attention from Washington City, as the nation's capital was then called. At the outset of the war, the sheriff of Oregon,

48

retired Rocky Mountain trapper Joseph Meek, was dispatched to Washington, D.C., where he presented himself as "envoy extraordinary and minister plenipotentiary from the Republic of Oregon to the Court of the United States." The "Court" was a sarcastic reference by Sheriff Meek to what he no doubt considered an effete and decadent capital compared to his own at Oregon City. This prejudice notwithstanding, Meek had come to request assistance in the Cayuse War and, in particular, to urge on President Polk, a shirttail relation, territorial status for the Oregon Country. Eventually, his efforts, along with others, would prove successful, but in the meantime, the second event so important to early Oregon had occurred.

One day in August of 1848, a Captain Newell sailed up the Willamette, buying all the spades he could find as he went along—a circumstance found puzzling. When his ship would hold no more of spades, wheat, and other provisions, Captain Newell informed the gulled locals that gold had been discovered in California.

It is estimated that two-thirds of the able-bodied men of Oregon threw down what was in hand—axes, awls, chisels, plows, pens, scales, forceps, tankards, Bibles—and departed for California. The most serious of the derelictions was the plow, for after all, the people left behind had to eat. The *Oregon Spectator* pled with Oregonians to stay on the farm until, that is, the paper's own printer departed, ending (for the time being) the paper's publication.

It is possible the Oregon settlement would not have survived, or if so but lamely, without the California gold rush. Now, for the first time, there was a nearby market for Oregon products. Also, many Oregonians returned with gold to replace what had been an awkward currency to say the least: wheat, one bushel one dollar.

Finally, there were those who, going off to the gold rush, never returned. Good riddance. Such could not be persons of worth, for otherwise, they would not have elected to remain in California. Here is Victor on the subject of the gold rush. "After all it will be seen that the distance of Oregon from the Sierra Foothills proved at this time the greatest of blessings, being near enough for commercial communication, and yet so far away as to escape the more evil consequences attending the mad scramble for wealth, such as social dissolutions, the rapine of intellect and principle, an overruling spirit of gambling—a delirium of development, attended by robbery,

[*continued on page* 52]

The introduction of steam-driven paddle-wheelers during the 1850s on the rivers of Oregon began a revolution in transport. Now, both cargo and passengers could move with relative ease on the Columbia and Willamette rivers and on many of their tributaries, due to the shallow draft of the river boats. The boats were also used for excursions to church picnics, lodge gatherings, baseball games, up the Columbia to see the falls, down the Columbia to see the waves. Also, their decks were much favored for balls and dances. Pictured here are the paddlewheelers *Oregona* and *Ruth* at Champoeg in 1907. (OHS neg. OrHi 12246)

According to California historian Hubert Howe Bancroft, in the California gold rush of 1848-49, miners from Oregon were known to be quick "with the rifle or the rope," and it is true that one of their first mining settlements was called Hangtown (today's Placerville near Sacramento). Whatever the truth of these unkind California allegations, the California mines and the later gold finds in southern and eastern Oregon contributed much to the early foundations of the Oregon economy. (From Francis Marryat's *Mountains & Molehills*, Harper & Bros., 1855. OHS neg. OrHi 4791)

50

"Stumptown," as it was commonly called, assumed
the far grander name of "City of Portland" (population about nine hundred) when it was incorporated in
1851. These pretensions were gradually realized as
more and more ships' masts (see photo) backdropped
the Front Street docks, and Portland became one of
the great wheat ports of the world. This photo shows
Portland's Front Avenue and Stark Street in 1852.
(OHS neg. OrHi 39197)

murder, and all uncleanness, and followed by reaction and death." From such wickedness Oregon, unlike its unfortunate neighbor to the south, had been preserved.

The third and last important happening in Oregon's 1840s was the culmination of the settlers' repeated requests for a United States presence. On 3 March 1849, Mexican War hero Joseph Lane of Indiana, appointed governor by President Polk, arrived in Oregon City to proclaim the Oregon Country an official territory of the United States.

At last, the settlers and their land were under United States protection. What stuck, however, in the craw of many was that they were also under United States authority. Heretofore, the people had enacted their own laws and elected their own officials. Hereafter, all principal officials could be appointed in Washington—political spoils, strangers ruling over Oregon. Also, the federal government might review and pass on Oregon legislation. The sop was one locally elected delegate to Congress. And the sop really fell short of even that, for the delegate had no vote. Finally, the settlers began to wonder if the protection itself was worth territorial status in view of the form that protection first took. This was the appearance in Oregon City, following Lane's arrival, of a United States force called the Mounted Rifle Regiment. According to Victor, they were "quartered at great expense, and to the disturbance of peace and order of that moral and temperate community." After a winter of racket, drunkenness, and random shots, they were removed to Fort Vancouver, a departure the citizens of Oregon City celebrated by burning down their barracks. Thus began the rather equivocal relations between the Territory of Oregon and the government of the United States.

"America is change," wrote Lord Bryce. Certainly, that was the case in the Oregon of the 1850s. Population at the beginning of the decade was thirteen thousand, at its end, fifty-two thousand. One result of this increase was that settlement spread from the Valley into the foothills: some of it in the bottoms of the tributary streams pouring down from the two mountain ranges, some higher up where the falling water could be utilized to power mills. The Valley floor itself was no longer burned over by the Indians, so the oak savannas multiplied, and here and there, invaders from the mountain slopes—groves of pointy firs. The greatest change, however, lay in the extent of cultivated land—wheat and oats, hay, potatoes, onions, the young orchards finally beginning to bear, all protected from the growing herds of cattle by the zigzag of split-rail fences.

Finally, now that there were mills, the crude cabins of chinked logs were giving way to the white simplicity of Greek Revival farmhouses, lilac at the door and inside, things almost unknown in the 1840s—a cookstove, a sewing machine, perhaps a settee and some fiddle-backed chairs brought around the Horn.

Growth and change were reflected in another significant development as well: the towns. By the middle of the decade, more than thirty had been registered in the Valley. There is hardly a Valley town today that does not have its origins in the 1850s. What is more, many of these towns were now linked, for by the middle 1850s, fourteen steamboats made scheduled runs on the Willamette. The towns themselves were not much, the buildings of a flimsy, slapdash sort, much clutter and muck about, but here and there, a columned courthouse went up. There was also the occasional academy where a youth might learn a little Latin and how to play the flute. As for the capital, one commentator wrote, "A sort of gay and fashionable air was imparted to Society in Oregon City by the families of the territorial officers . . . which was a new thing in the Willamette Valley, and provoked not a little jealousy among the more sedate and surly."

There was development as well at both ends of the Valley. In 1850, gold was discovered in the Rogue River valley which led to the founding of Jacksonville, to which Ashland supplied lumber and flour. Roseburg had its beginnings in 1852 as a waystation on the Oregon-California immigrant trail. It was, however, at the other end of the Valley, at the Willamette's final bend, that the most impressive developments occurred.

Portland's dream began in 1845, sixteen blocks platted out along the river bank and a coin flipped to give the place the name of Portland. Two advantages vouchsafed Portland the eventual edge over the other river towns. It was the head of navigation, the farthest point on the river to which ocean-going ships could proceed at all seasons of the year. Thus were the upriver towns of Milwaukie, Gladstone, and Oregon City cut out.

On the other hand, Portland had a low-grade pass—the route of present Canyon Road and Highway 26—built through the hills to the rich wheatlands of the Tualatin valley. Thus were downriver towns such as Linnton and St. Helens cut out, for their accesses to the Valley were over prohibitive-

[*continued on page* 56]   53

To avoid the slavery question, the territorial legislature passed the exclusion law of 1849 prohibiting black immigration to Oregon—permitting those already here to remain. A. H. Francis arrived in Portland after passage of the law; despite his illegal status, he opened one of the city's principal establishments (pictured here in 1858). He was aided by two hundred Portlanders who petitioned the legislature to exempt him from the exclusion law. (OHS neg. OrHi 9715)

The churches were great centers of social life in early Oregon—benefits, dinners, picnics, and in particular, the choirs where the two sexes praised the Lord and cast appraising glances. Pictured here is the seventeen-member Congregational Church choir of Portland, 1855. (OHS neg. CN 017846)

A nationally known jurist, Judge Matthew Deady figured largely on the Oregon scene from his arrival in 1849 until his death in 1893. After presiding over the state constitutional convention in 1857, he was appointed United States District Judge for Oregon. He was also one of the founders of the Multnomah County Public Library and served for twenty years as a regent of the University of Oregon. His diaries, edited by Malcolm Clark and published in two volumes by the Oregon Historical Society Press, provide a detailed and fascinating record of Oregon life in the last decades of the nineteenth century. (OHS neg. OrHi 9506)

At the time of the Rogue River Indian wars of 1853-56, Indians approached the Harris homestead with what appeared to be hostile intent. George Harris shot one of the Indians and then was shot himself. Armed with a rifle, revolver, and shotgun, while her eleven-year-old daughter molded bullets, Mary Ann Young Harris held off the Indians for many hours until the arrival of troops. (OHS neg. CN 010834)

55

ly steep grades. In short, Portland was a place where the wagons could meet the ships, and during the California gold rush, many wagons met many ships. With wheat and gold, the wharf and the road, sawmill, tannery, blacksmith shop, and a population of about eight hundred, Portland was, as a local judge described it, "a small and beautiful village." In fact, it was a raw, disheveled place, gangling and awkward in the spurt of its first growth. "Rather gamey," said a woman passing through on her way south.

By 1851, however, the town was incorporated. A brick building with arches went up at the waterfront, Classic Revival cottages with tiny pillared porches appeared on the now elm-planted blocks, land was set aside for parks, and there was a "library," and a music shop. By 1858, there were one hundred stores and a population of about two thousand. Oregon had its "metropolis."

Portland, Oregon City, and the smaller river towns, in these were centered Oregon's trade and commerce, but they were also centers of something else—faction. As a California journalist of the time wrote, "The Oregonians have two occupations, agriculture and politics." This interest in politics arose in part from the fact that in the nineteenth century, politics could be about as dear to a man as life, and in part from the fact that politics was the trough in which the slop of spoils flowed. It was the crowding at this trough that accounts for the rough and tumble of Oregon politics in the decade of the 1850s.

The principal contestants in the mêlée were the Democrats, the Whigs (predecessors of the Republicans), the Temperance party, and the Know Nothings, the latter a secret society of nativists out to foul Roman Catholics, the foreign-born, and the Democrats. The Democrats were the majority party and tended to be agrarian in membership, whereas their principal adversaries, the Whigs, were town-oriented. The two parties disagreed over just about everything except their desire for spoils and voiced their disagreement loudly and abusively in their respective papers, the Whig *Oregonian* and the Democratic *Oregon Statesman*. The latter referred to the *Oregonian* as "the Sewer" and on one occasion, stigmatized it as "a complete tissue of gross profanity, obscenity, falsehood and meanness" whose editor seldom told the truth "even by mistake." Editor Dryer of the *Oregonian* responded by labeling Editor Bush of the *Statesman*, "pimp generalissimo of a small, cheap paper."

One of the main issues on which the two parties disagreed was the location of the state capital, a controversy that raged for some fifteen years. Initially at Oregon City, it was moved to Salem, then to Marysville (now, Corvallis), then back again to Salem, where a statehouse was finally completed, only to be set on fire.

Another serious issue was statehood. The Democrats favored it since, as the majority party, they could be sure of capturing the elective offices as well as patronage. The Whigs (by 1857, the Republicans) opposed it for the same reasons. The people on the whole were not interested, not sure by any means they wished to join the Union, and on three occasions voted the proposition down. Finally, due mainly to the will and work of the Democratic party machine, the measure was carried, and on 15 March 1859, the *Brother Jonathan* sailed into Portland with the news Oregon had become the thirty-third state on 14 February.

The 1850s in Oregon were a decade of growth and also of refinement of what was at hand. There was achievement in all areas—the economy, transportation, education, government, and the amenities of everyday life. But overlaying all of this there was a stain, and it was the stain of blood. From 1851-53, and again from 1855-56, Indian wars plagued both southern and northeastern Oregon.

The problem was land. With the Donation Land Law of 1850, Congress offered free land to the immigrants before arranging for its purchase from the natives—treaty after treaty later negotiated for such a purpose but none ratified. Some of the settlers sympathized with the Indians in their plight, but many urged their extermination. "Indeed, this seems to be the only alternative left," editorialized the *Oregonian* in the fall of 1853. Certain individuals took it upon themselves to do just that, but others, such as Joseph Lane and Joel Palmer, sought to gain fair treatment for the natives. Palmer, superintendent of Indian affairs, 1853-56, initiated the reservation system in Oregon as a means of protecting the natives from the whites and to bring peace to the two races. In a limited way, his policy was effective, but it was not to be the end of Indian hostilities.

6

The Valley & Beyond

Though proudly independent and often critical of the federal government and its claims, Oregon remained Unionist during the Civil War. There were pockets of Oregonians sympathetic to the South and slavery, but their support was limited to such acts as throwing the Albany municipal cannon into the river so it could not be fired to celebrate Lincoln's election. By and large, Oregon was little touched by the war; its attention concentrated instead on an event and region far closer to home, the discovery of gold in eastern Oregon, Idaho, and Montana.

Eastern Oregon had not created a favorable first impression. "The plains smoked with dust and dearth," remarked Thomas Farnham in 1839. A later immigrant agreed. "This is a barren, God-forsaken country, fit for nothing but to receive the footprints of the savage and his universal associate the coyote." Yet only eight years later, a process began—summarized by D. W. Meinig as "gold, grass and grain"—that was to make the interior one of the richest regions in the new state.

The gold strikes themselves, in 1861 and 1862 in Baker and Grant counties, were enormously lucrative, an estimated $20 million taken from the mines in 1862 alone. As with the previous strikes in California in the 1840s and in southern Oregon in the 1850s, the economy of the whole state benefited immensely from this infusion.

Of more permanent importance was the fact that cattle began to be driven across the Cascades from the Valley to feed the miners—more than one

[*continued on page* 64]   59

The arrival of sheep in Oregon in the 1840s was of momentous importance for, with the exception of hides, there was no other local material for clothing. The first woolen mill was opened in Oregon City in 1857. Others followed in Brownsville, Ellendale, Salem, Ashland, and, with the movement of sheep beyond the Cascades, at The Dalles and Pendleton. In time, wool and garment manufacturing became one of Oregon's principal industries. The S. G. Reed farm near Reedsville is pictured. (OHS neg. OrHi 42778)

Threshing wheat from dawn to dusk was hot and dirty work. Not shown here are the attendant water wagons and mobile cookhouses that provided occasional respite to these crews (near Moro) in their grueling labors. (Raymond photo. OHS neg. OrHi 6337)

60

Cattle ranching in central and eastern Oregon has long been one of the most important elements in the state's economy. This photo was taken at the Herman Oliver ranch near Seneca. (Photo courtesy Ray Atkeson. OHS neg. OrHi 25179)

"Gandy dancers" were the workers who laid railroad ties, and the "dance" was said to be the motions made while doing so. The origin of "gandy" is obscure but is possibly from Hindu. Large numbers of Chinese were employed as gandy dancers. Here, a group of gandy dancers, from the Pacific Railroad Company of Corvallis and eastern Oregon, ride a handcar. (OHS neg. OrHi 50082)

As early as the 1850s, barrels of salted salmon were shipped out in large quantities from Astoria. By the 1870s with the introduction of tin containers, there were more than a dozen canneries on the lower river. In addition to gill-netting, seining for salmon was common. The nets, as shown here, were pulled to shore by horses. (OHS neg. OrHi 49091)

The Rogue River Indian wars were among the bloodiest of the nation's Indian-white conflicts. Originating in terrorists' attacks by both white miners and Rogue River Indians, the wars raged from 1853-56. After their conclusion, the Rogues, along with other southern Oregon and coastal tribes, were confined to reservations where conditions were far from ideal. And it was this that prompted Chief John's (pictured here) famous charge: "It is not your war but your peace which has killed my people." (OHS neg. OrHi 4355)

An impediment to travel on the upper river, the Cascades of the Columbia required a portage. In 1859, a rail portage was built on the south bank, and here ran the Oregon Pony, the state's first locomotive. The north-side portage, shown here in 1867, was constructed during the 1860s. The blockhouse, upper left, was erected to provide protection. (C. E. Watkins photo. OHS neg. OrHi 21109)

Before the time of power saws, logging was "labor intensive," as this photo suggests. (OHS neg. OrHi 35995)

hundred thousand head in the decade of the 1860s. It was at this time that grazing land was growing short in the Valley, whereas in the interior, there was an abundance of bunchgrass, not to mention the wild rye and flax and meadow grass of the bottoms. Here were later born the great cattle empires of Oregon with their barons, men like Pete French and Henry Miller, and so, too, the beginnings of cattle towns—Burns, Prineville, Lakeview, and others.

Cattle were followed by sheep with consequences that in time would prove lamentable. Great sheep empires were created as well, most of these in northeastern Oregon between The Dalles and the Umatilla River. These, too, contributed much to the founding and growth of towns like Happner, Pendleton, and Condon. In this region, also, was the Hay Creek Ranch, largest merino breeding station in the world. Not far away was Shaniko which at one point, when the railroad came, handled more wool than any railhead in the world. It was the railroad, too, that carried sheep-raising into southeastern Oregon. This gradual encroachment by the sheepmen and their close-cropping flocks upon the cattle ranges led to the sheep and cattle wars, which were not settled until the present century and in which thousands of sheep and cattle, and some men as well, were shot.

Many factors brought about the relative decline of the sheep and cattle business. The Valley, with its late springs, had never been entirely ideal for the raising of wheat, whereas the high country, particularly in the northeast with its warmer climate but moisture-holding soil, seemed meant for wheat. It was a suitability, however, that could not be realized until the railroads of the 1880s made possible cheap, convenient transportation. When that happened, it was an increasingly apparent matter of economics. More money could be made from an acre sown than an acre grazed. In 1869, the first wheat shipment went to Liverpool. By 1890, a grain ship left Portland for foreign ports on the average of once a week.

Thus the development of the interior, "gold, grass and grain." By the turn of the century—with its sixteen counties, dozens of towns, its wheat, cattle, sheep, and still here and there some gold—the interior had come into its own, enriching and broadening a state that for so long had lived both literally and figuratively in that narrowness called "the Valley."

No region could be in greater contrast to the high country of the interior than the Oregon coast. Though the first region to be visited by whites, it was the last to be developed, in part because of its isolation. The waters off the Oregon coast are among the roughest in the world. Furthermore, there are few harbors, and those few are obstructed by dangerous bars. Inland are the mountains which, until the recent era of good roads, were difficult to cross except in summer. The remainder of the year the passes were deep in snow and mud. In the Valley and in areas of the interior, good agricultural land abounded, whereas on the coast there was little. Finally, during those years when so much development was taking place in the interior, the entire central Oregon coast was closed because it had been set aside as an Indian reservation.

In the beginning, and for many years thereafter, what development occurred tended to take place at the northern and southern ends of the coast. Following the removal of the Hudson's Bay Company to Fort Vancouver in 1824, Astoria languished until the late 1840s when immigrants began to settle there. In 1864, the first salmon canning factory was established, and from then on, Astoria served as the center of the industry. Not long after, Ben Holladay, the railroad entrepreneur, built the luxurious Sea Side House in present Seaside, and the northern coast began its years as a popular resort.

Tillamook was settled early as well. It was the site of the first American landing on the Oregon coast, by Captain Robert Gray on his initial voyage in 1788. He, however, called it Murderer's Bay because it was here his black cabin boy, Markus Lopius, was killed by local natives. The first Euro-American settler was Joseph Champion, who arrived in 1851 and made his home in a tree he referred to as his "castle." Tillamook's growth was slow. Not until 1871 was there a road of sorts to the Valley and not until 1884 did a stage begin to run. Scandinavians, drawn in part by the fishing, now began to predominate on the coast—large numbers of Finns, for example, at Astoria—but at Tillamook and a few other places, Swiss settled and developed a cheese-making industry.

South of Tillamook the Siletz Indian Reservation began, the reservation established by Joel Palmer in the 1850s for the several thousand displaced natives of southern Oregon and the Willamette Valley. It extended 125 miles down the coast and from the sea to the mountains, roughly 1,300,000 acres. Forty years later, it had been reduced to 47,000 acres, and of the natives, there were only a few hundred left. Disease, famine, and greed had done their work.

[*continued on page 74*] 65

The Oregon coast has long been known as one of the most treacherous in the world, partly because of the turbulence of its waters, partly because of the number of its promontories. It was to warn passing ships of the latter that lighthouse building began in 1857 and continued throughout the century. Pictured are the Cape Meares lighthouse and attendant. (OHS neg. OrHi 37823)

After appropriating Siletz Reservation lands at Newport in 1865, entrepreneurs built Oregon's first resort hotel, the Ocean House (pictured). At the same time, the Corvallis and Yaquina Bay Wagon Road Company began operating a stage from Corvallis over the mountains to Newport, a distance of forty-five miles. Thus began what is today a principal feature of the economy of the Oregon coast. (OHS neg OrHi 28046)

Resorts in early Oregon had much to do with water. Certain kinds of water were thought to be highly therapeutic, tonic both to drink and bathe in. Thus, many of these early resorts were at the various hot springs scattered through the mountains. But salt-water, too—as well as salt air—was thought to be beneficial to the constitution. Thus, the coast also was the locale of many early resorts. (OHS neg. OrHi 24901)

At the time this photo was taken (circa 1900), Portland was one of the great wheat ports of the world. The port is still the largest exporter of grain on the West Coast. (OHS neg. Oreg. 418)

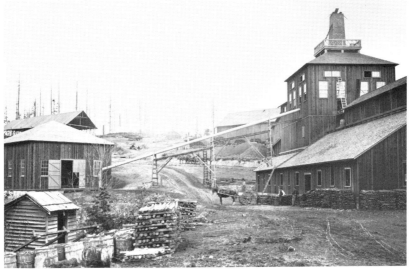

Hoping to become the "Pittsburgh of the West," Oswego began to smelt iron ore in 1867. In 1908 however, and after many vicissitudes, the blast furnaces closed down and Oswego became instead a placid suburb built around a lake, its smelter green with ivy. (C. E. Watkins photo. OHS neg. OrHi 21593)

Early prisons were regularly burned down. The first to remain intact was located in Portland. Among its first inmates were Nimrod O'Kelly who shot one Jeramiah Mahoney who had "intruded on his land," and Charity Lamb who, infatuated with a neighbor, axed her husband to death while he was having dinner. The prison was moved to Salem in 1866. Here, convicts are at work in a Salem rock quarry. (OHS neg. CN 0172 G 050)

The first immigration of Chinese to Oregon came by way of the California and Oregon mines during the 1850s. In the 1870s and 1880s, many more came directly to Oregon from China to work on the four railroads then under construction in the state. By the last decades of the century, Portland's Chinese community was the second largest in the nation. The Chinese Exclusion Act of 1882, together with prejudice against the Chinese during times of high unemployment, greatly reduced their numbers. Pictured here is Mr. Lung An after his arrival in John Day. (OHS neg. OrHi 53840)

Pictured here is a view of Sixth and Yamhill in Portland circa 1877-78. The house in the foreground
belonged to the Corbett family and was not razed
until the 1930s. It was known in later years as "the
million dollar cow pasture" because of the cow that
Mrs. Corbett pastured on the property. The house in
the background belonged to the Failing family. There
were a number of private houses downtown through
the early decades of this century. (Wertzen photo.
OHS neg OrHi 759)

Willamette University, some of whose students are pictured here, has the distinction of being Oregon's—indeed the West's—oldest institution of higher learning, founded in 1842. The first public institutions were Oregon State University in 1868 and the University of Oregon in 1876. Both were located in small towns in the central Willamette Valley partly because the population of the Valley was greater than Portland's and, perhaps, partly because of the nineteenth-century view that cities tended to corrupt the young. (Thomas Cronise photo. OHS neg. CN 0172 G 026)

Normal schools were enormously important institutions in nineteenth- and early twentieth-century Oregon. Existing at various times in Eugene, Monmouth, Ashland, Weston, La Grande, Drain, and The Dalles, their graduates went out to teach at the hundreds of town and country schoolhouses throughout the state. The State Normal School in Drain is pictured. (OHS neg. OrHi 82067)

Originally known as Wascopum, The Dalles was a great center of the tribes of the upper Columbia. Its present name came from French Canadian trappers. White settlement began with the establishment of a Methodist mission in 1838. The Dalles boomed in the 1860s due to the eastern Oregon and Idaho gold fields and continued to prosper when it became the major wheat-shipping port on the Columbia. The city is pictured here in 1867. (OHS neg. OrHi 21578)

Fruit growing began in Oregon in 1847 when Henderson Luelling arrived by wagon train in Milwaukie with ten children and seven hundred fruit scions. Later, the Hood River valley and the Medford region became world famous for the quality of their fruit. (OHS neg. Gi 1105)

72

An early schoolroom. (OHS neg. OrHi 56093)

A typical rowdy Willamette Valley town, Dallas was originally built mainly of wood in the humble form of the Classic Revival style. Few of these early Valley structures remain, many of them lost to fire. This photo is Dallas circa 1874. (Photo courtesy Polk County Historical Society. OHS neg. OrHi 81793)

The first bite out of these Indian lands was taken in 1865 at what is now Newport. The year before, oysters, for which there was a ravenous market in the grillrooms and saloons of San Francisco, had been found in great numbers in Yaquina Bay. Two years later in 1866, a regular stage began to operate on the new military road from Corvallis to the coast at present Newport where the Ocean House, a resort hotel, was built. Newport was on its way.

Certain areas of the southern coast, like the northern coast, were early populated—the former because of sea otter pelts, "soft gold," the latter because of hard gold, the real stuff. Both Port Orford and Gold Beach began in the early 1850s as mining communities, the latter aptly named since grains of gold and grains of sand were literally intermixed there at the mouth of the Rogue River. These communities also drew population because of the Rogue River Indian wars of the 1850s—and lost population, too. It was at Gold Beach that one of the worst incidents of the wars took place, the Rogue River Indians murdering twenty-three whites, among them the controversial Indian agent, Ben Wright, whose heart they cooked and ate while his men danced at a ball. However, the southern coast community that was to know the greatest growth did not trace its origins to wars and gold but to settlement and the good use of its port and timbered hinterland. This was Coos Bay, for years the largest lumber shipping port in the world. There was as well Ross Hume's salmon fisheries at Rogue River.

Finally, one other kind of development took place on the coast that must not be overlooked. In 1863, during the Civil War, Fort Stevens was constructed. For the next eighty-four years, it remained the principal guardian of the Columbia. It was also in these last decades of the nineteenth century those nine structures were built that symbolize as well as anything the Oregon coast—its lighthouses.

Despite the little resorts and the industries—lumber, salmon, oysters, cheese and other dairy products—the coast at the turn of the century remained an isolated, largely undeveloped place, far more so than the interior. It was to remain so until the 1930s when good, hard-surfaced roads finally made it over the mountains from the Valley, and in particular, with the completion in 1933 of the Coast Highway, which before had been in many places simply the beach when the tide was out. Yet this delayed development of the coast has been a great boon to Oregon, for now, with public ownership of the beaches and more than fifty percent of the ocean-front land in public hands, few scenic coasts in the world are better preserved and protected.

If development was slow at the coast, it was not so in the Valley, particularly at Portland. The gold finds and Indian wars of the 1850s in southern Oregon had stimulated its economy considerably, but it was the gold finds of the 1860s east of the Cascades that really filled the Portland pocket. This good fortune was followed by another in the following decade—wheat. Beginning in the 1870s, Portland was on its way to becoming one of the major wheat ports of the world.

With these economic changes came others as well. Like any thriving city, Portland attracted foreign immigrants—Irish, German, Jewish, Scottish, Scandinavian, Chinese—grafts on the American stock that had founded the town. Also, that white and wooden New England look was passing and had been replaced by stone and brick and the prefabricated splendor of cast-iron fronts. Likewise, the classical cottages of the neighborhoods were here and there giving way to the bay-windowed "mansions" in the Italian Villa style. The walls of these grander houses were often hung with the trophies of European tours, for Portland was no longer "rather gamey" as the woman bound for California had so unkindly said. By the 1870s the town, having survived two major conflagrations, boasted an opera house, several theaters, a library, a concert orchestra, and four academies. Culture had arrived.

It had arrived in other places, too. Salem, Forest Grove, Albany, Corvallis, McMinnville, and Eugene all had their colleges by the 1870s. Literary societies were popular in many places, and libraries had been established in all the major Valley towns. Like Portland, these towns had their touches of grandness too: Gothic castle or Italian villa taking up the whole of an elm-lined block, an opera house perhaps, almost certainly a large, impressive hotel (the sign in the last decades of the century that a town had "arrived").

The basis of all this thriving townlife was, of course, the farmland of the Willamette Valley. Until the middle of the 1870s, wheat continued to be the major crop, but now, too, flax and, in particular, hops began to be cultivated while better transportation encouraged the raising of more perishable produce such as fruits and vegetables.

The most visible changes, however, were in the landscape itself. With the invention of barbed wire in the 1870s, rail fences began to disappear. Farm

[*continued on page* 84]

That the early pioneers on occasion took Indian
women as mates is often forgotten or not known.
A close examination of this photograph (taken in
Aurora, 1874) is instructive. (OHS neg. OrHi 25868)

Thomas Lamb Eliot came to Oregon as a Unitarian minister in 1867. During his remaining seven decades in Portland, he did more than anyone in the city's history to promote education and philanthropy. In addition to his clerical duties and his duties as director of the Portland Library Association and Superintendent of Schools, he was the principal founder of the parks system, the Humane Society, the Boys and Girls Aid Society, and Reed College. Mt. Hood's Eliot glacier is named for him because he was an ardent mountaineer and was responsible for opening up the mountain's northern slopes for recreation. There hardly could be a better example than Thomas Lamb Eliot of the Skidmore Fountain's dictum, "Good citizens are the riches of a city." Eliot is pictured here as a young man and as he was in 1932. (OHS negs. OrHi 4213 & 82629, the latter is from Earl Morse Wilbur's *Thomas Lamb Eliot, 1841-1936*, Portland, Oregon: G.M. Allen & Son, 1937)

The first community structure built by the pioneers
was often a church which sometimes, as in this case,
was sited atop an oak knoll overlooking the surround-
ing countryside. There are now, perhaps, less than a
dozen of these 1850s churches remaining in the
Willamette Valley. In the simplicity and purity of their
design, they are among the state's most beautiful
buildings, with their adjacent graveyards strongly
evoking the pioneer past. Pictured here is the Spring
Valley Presbyterian Church in Zena, Polk County.
(OHS neg. OrHi 56770)

The first Indian manual labor school was founded by Jason Lee at Mission Bottom on the Willamette in 1834. It was not successful. A second, pictured here in 1882, was started in Forest Grove in 1880 but was moved to Salem in 1886. The purpose of these schools, as their name implies, was to teach young Indians a trade. But as boarding schools were distant from the students' families, it was also hoped the students would abandon their native ways and languages. (Davidson photo. OHS neg. OrHi 4456)

Matrimony. (OHS neg. OrHi 82069)

Mountain climbing has been an Oregon diversion
since Joel Palmer ascended the southern slopes of Mt.
Hood in 1845. In 1857 a party of four, their faces veiled
and blackened with burnt cork, reached the summit.
Then in 1894 the Mazamas, one of the country's oldest
and most distinguished alpine clubs, was founded.
The event was celebrated by a mass ascent of Hood
through sleet and the thunder of two hundred enthusi-
asts. Mountain climbing is now general throughout
Oregon. Here, a group of climbers ascend Mt.
Ashland. (OHS neg. OrHi 55615)

A six-day work week and no paid vacations was the norm in the nineteenth and early twentieth centuries. Also, most people's work involved fairly strenuous physical labor. Accordingly, the highly popular Sunday picnic was a time for repose and relaxation. (OHS neg. OrHi 6476)

In the nineteenth and early twentieth centuries, no community would have dared call itself a town if it lacked a band. These bands were much in demand, not only for Sundays in the park, but also for the frequent processions and parades so favored during the period. Pictured here is the Popcorn Band of Salem. (OHS neg. CN 0166 G 010)

Today's bicycle dates from the 1890s when chain drives and pneumatic-tired wheels became fully practical. Thereafter, biking for transportation as well as pleasure became the rage. They were particularly favored for a group "spin" in the countryside. (OHS neg OrHi 39197)

Though unattached individuals existed in nineteenth-century Oregon, they were rare compared with the present. Almost everyone was a member of, and lived with, a family. It was not uncommon for children, parents, a grandparent, perhaps an aunt or uncle, and a cousin or two all to live under one roof. (OHS neg. OrHi 76508)

Baseball was *the* team sport of nineteenth-century Oregon. Every town had its team and the games were a principal diversion—more than a diversion when the "contest" turned into a "conflict," as sometimes happened. Animosity between the towns involved could last for decades. (Thomas Cronise photo. OHS neg. CN 0038 G 070)

Late nineteenth-century Portland, looking north on Broadway from Madison Avenue. (OHS neg OrHi 20684-a)

machinery called for larger barns and larger fields as well. Roads had greatly improved. The lone rider was still to be seen—a politician on his rounds, a preacher on his circuit, a young man a-courting, a woman bound for camp-meeting, the children up behind—but far more common now were the buckboard and the surrey. One-room schoolhouses were everywhere, and there were the little country churches, often crowning a hilltop in a grove of oak, the few that remain today among the most touching and beautiful remnants of early Oregon life. There were, too, beginning in the 1880s, those most emblematic of rural structures—the Grange halls. Finally, and like the churches often situated on a little rise, there was a feature that more than any other reflected change and the passing of time, and specifically the passing of the pioneer era—the graveyards. Each year, more and more headstones marked the journey's end for those who had set out across the plains in the middle decades of the nineteenth century, and who, with their dreams and work, began to form the place that is Oregon today.

Some, of course, were still alive, for having survived the trail, they tended to die old. One day in the autumn of 1883, fifty pioneers gathered in Portland to lead a parade. The purpose of the parade was to honor the end of their era and to celebrate the beginning of another, for behind the old men steamed a transcontinental locomotive, the first to reach Oregon.

7

Passing of the Past

Since settlement, no single event did more to transform Oregon than did the railroads. The first, promoted by Ben Holladay in 1868, was to link Portland with San Francisco. By 1872, it had reached Roseburg and thus, by that date, was the Valley served. With the arrival in 1883 of that first transcontinental train in Portland and the completion of Holladay's line to San Francisco in 1887, Portland was, as the president of the Portland Board of Trade put it, "incorporated with the rest of the world." In the next years, local lines were constructed to the coast, across the interior, and all through the Valley. By the turn of the century Oregon, excepting the southeast corner, was fully integrated by its rails.

A number of consequences followed. Now, agriculture was no longer limited to areas served by water routes. In the interior, the railroads affected the transition from a cattle-raising economy to one of wheat and wool. The coast at Astoria, Newport, and Coos Bay was relieved, to some degree, of its isolation. New towns developed at important junctions, and more than one county seat was moved so as to be closer to the locomotives' toot. Portland, where all rails met, became more than ever the economic center of the state. Finally, the railroads facilitated immigration to Oregon from all regions of the country.

There was, however, one consequence of the railroads not foreseen or, at any rate, not desired: the high freight rates. For farmers, these could be prohibitive. Efforts to lower them were initially defeated due to the alliance

[*continued on page* 90]   85

Along with steam-powered river boats, mechanized farm machinery, and automobiles, railroads had a massive impact on the development of Oregon. Pictured is a locomotive station in Oregon City, 1888. (Harley C. Stevens photo. OHS neg. OrHi 13375)

Described by historian Malcolm Clark as an "accomplished lawyer, politician, scalawag and womanizer," John H. Mitchell began his Oregon career in Portland city government in 1860. He then moved on to the state senate and from there to Washington, D.C., in 1873. In Washington, despite his flagrant dishonesty and sexual transgressions, Mitchell served as Republican senator from Oregon for a total of twenty-two years. (Strohmey and Wyman photo. OHS neg. OrHi 26849)

The Mazamas, an Oregon alpine club founded in 1894, combined scientific enquiry with mountain climbing. Here, in British Columbia, they are attempting to heliograph messages—by way of mirrors and the sun—to Mexico. (OHS neg. OrHi 26124)

Sylvester Pennoyer, an 1854 Harvard Law School graduate, came to Oregon the following year. He began his career teaching school, went into the lumber business, edited a newspaper, was elected governor in 1886 and mayor of Portland in 1896. He was one of Oregon's most outspoken and eccentric political figures. Once, he lectured President Grover Cleveland in a telegram which read: "I will attend to my business, let the President attend to his." (OHS neg. OrHi 54772)

William S. U'Ren, principal author of the "Oregon System" of political reform, had a varied past before entering Oregon political life. Growing up in the West, he worked as a miner, blacksmith, newspaper editor, fruit farmer, and spiritualist's medium. A dedicated reformer, he had, as Stewart Holbrook wrote, "tremendous influence on his time." (OHS neg. OrHi 81789)

Abigail Scott Duniway began her career as a teacher in the Salem area in 1853. She later worked in Albany as a milliner. In 1871, she moved to Portland to become one of the country's principal proponents of woman's rights. In addition to lecturing nation-wide, her newspaper, the *New Northwest*, carried her message throughout the West. Her career was capped in 1912 when she was seventy-eight and woman suffrage became law in Oregon. Here, she signs the Equal Suffrage Proclamation while Governor Oswald West and Dr. Viola Coe look on. (*Oregonian* photo. OHS neg. Oreg 4590)

In the nineteenth century, before the time of movies, radio, and television, amateur theatricals were a major form of recreation for both the players and audiences. Granges, schools, churches, clubs, and informal groups brought theater to every part of the state. (OHS neg. OrHi 82068)

In 1890, having completed a B.A. and M.A. in Greek studies at Oberlin College, Eva Emery Dye and her husband, an attorney, came to live in Oregon City. While rearing her four children, she began to write— "when my children were in sight I always wrote better . . . some of my best work has been done when there was considerable noise around me." Her substantial output of historical novels and stories was based on the interviews she did with the surviving pioneers and Indians of the region. Here, she is taking notes from an Indian woman who remembered Lewis and Clark. (OHS neg. OrHi 4331)

between the railroads and government. In the last decades of the century, government in Oregon was largely in the hands of the colorful but conservative wing of the Republican party. The color came from such figures as John H. Mitchell and George Williams, both flamboyantly venal and both United States senators. When Mitchell, for example, died in office in 1905, he had been convicted of both bigamy and bribery. It was in response to such escapades, but in particular to the freight rates, that the first but unsuccessful protests were mounted by the new Oregon Grange in the 1870s.

In time, the protest movement broadened its base to include small businessmen as well as farmers, conservatives as well as liberals. Much of this protest was expressed through the new political party called the Populists. With the election of the Populist candidate, Sylvester Pennoyer, to the governorship in 1886, reform achieved a significant victory. With the appearance of the Progressive, William S. U'Ren and his Direct Legislation League in 1898, political corruption was finally at bay.

U'Ren believed reform could only be achieved by citizens taking a more direct role in legislation. To this end, U'Ren and his supporters succeeded in passing the initiative and referendum bills in 1902, the direct primary in 1904, an effective corrupt practices act in 1908, and in 1910, the recall. Thus was the Oregon System of direct participation by the electorate completed—a model subsequently adopted by many other states.

This was as well a period of progressive labor legislation, though labor organization began in Oregon in 1853 with the creation of the Typographical Society. The Portland Protection Union, which was the second union organized in the state, was formed in 1868. By the 1880s, there were some twenty trade unions, the American Federation of Labor appearing in Portland in 1887. The reform period in the first years of the twentieth century saw the enactment in 1913 of a worker's compensation law and the first effective minimum wage and maximum hour law for women in the nation. The reform movement's concern for women had also been expressed the previous year when a suffrage amendment was finally added to the state constitution.

It was in this rush of reform that Oregon left the old century and entered the next, almost all segments of society affected by the new provisions. One group, as usual, was not touched by these improvements: the native Oregonians.

The reservation system had not proved a solution to "the Indian problem." Bands hostile to each other were often placed on the same reserve. Government administrators could be corrupt and incompetent. The natives were encouraged to farm on land that in many instances was unsuited to agriculture. The Modoc War of 1872 south of Klamath, the Nez Perce War of 1877 in northeastern Oregon, and the Bannock War of 1878 in southeastern Oregon (the last of the Indian wars), all arose out of resistance to reservation life. In 1887, the Dawes Act abolished the natives' communal ownership of their reservation, giving them individual parcels instead, with the hope this would encourage them to be independent farmers. The principal result of the act was an enormous reduction in the amount of Indian-held land. As Gordon Dodds has written, "By the 1880s Oregon Indians, for the white majority, were literally out-of-sight and out-of-mind, consigned to fringe regions, unworthy in their impotence even of hatred."

Excepting, then, the status of native Oregonians, it was with a bang of reform that Oregon entered the twentieth century. It entered with another bang as well, or more accurately, a bash, indeed a colossal bash: the Lewis and Clark Centennial and American Pacific Exposition and Oriental Fair of 1905. First promoted by the Oregon Historical Society, the purpose of this international exposition was to celebrate the centenary of the arrival of the two intrepid explorers and their party, the first official United States presence in the West. There was another motive as well: visitors, overwhelmed by paradise, might settle and invest.

Laid out near the river in northwest Portland, the fair was said to be a "scene of unparalleled splendor": the flowing turf and balustraded terraces, a sunken garden, stately staircases descending to a lake, a cornucopia of agricultural produce, the flywheels of a hundred new inventions, exotic gewgaws from the East, lots of roses and electric lights—Eden up-to-date. The fair, with its nearly three million visitors, was an enormous success. Though not the only factor, the fair did play an important part in Portland's population leap. In 1900 a good-sized town of ninety thousand, it was by 1910 a city of two hundred thousand while the state itself now approached seven hundred thousand.

One feature of the fair was prophetic. It served as the terminus for the country's first transcontinental auto race. The automobile had come and with it the beginning of changes that would outstrip even those of the

[*continued on page* 100]   91

Henry Wemme, Portland businessman and benefactor
of unwed mothers, brought the first automobile to
Oregon in 1899. Throughout the next decade, the
contraption caused much confusion as is apparent
above (in Albany). There were more serious consequences as well. An auto speeding at thirty miles per
hour down Washington Street in Portland was
ordered by a police officer to stop. When the occupants refused to do so, the officer fired two shots. The
occupants returned fire and proceeded on down the
street. (OHS neg. OrHi 202)

BIRD'S EYE VIEW OF LEWIS AND CLARK CENTENNIAL EXPOSITION AND ORIENTAL FAIR
PORTLAND, OREGON

Despite the "flowing turf and balustraded terraces" and all the roses, one observer described the Lewis and Clark Exposition of 1905 as "gaudy, rowdy and smelly." He may well have meant the Exposition's midway which featured "graceful and supple Oriental dancers," a Temple of Mirth, a village of aboriginal "dog eaters" (like Lewis and Clark themselves), a life-size cow molded in butter, and a rather desiccated Egyptian mummy. There were also many mosquitoes. (OHS neg. OrHi 28279)

Rafting logs (left) was a common and relatively cheap method of transporting logs from forest to mills and market. Simon Benson, an early Oregon lumberman, devised a new method of chain-linking the timber that was so successful he was able to run ocean-going rafts of five million board feet as far as San Diego. (OHS neg. OrHi 21754)

In the nineteenth century the Fourth of July, not Christmas, was the major holiday of the year. It was celebrated with balls, picnics, the reading of the Constitution, lengthy orations, innumerable toasts (with "Adam's ale," i.e., water, during times of Prohibition), fireworks, and most importantly, parades. In many places the celebration of the Fourth lasted for several days. Pictured is a parade in Silverton, Oregon. (Drake photo. OHS neg. OrHi 13627)

Begun in 1907, the Portland Rose Festival is one of the nation's oldest civic festivals. Queens were chosen in various fashions until 1930, when she was selected from among Portland high school princesses. The annual June parade is the occasion for Portlanders to come together to celebrate their city and its symbol, the rose. (OHS neg. OrHi 82628)

In the first decade of the twentieth century, apartment houses began to be built in Oregon. Until then, and for some years thereafter, boarding and rooming houses—from the exclusive to the seedy—were the usual housing for many people, especially the young but families as well. These establishments, like the Marquam rooming house of Portland pictured here, were often in the center of town. (OHS neg. CN 010129)

For generations of Portlanders, the apex of the year was a summer's afternoon spent at Oaks Park. Amusement parks were much favored in the early years of the twentieth century. In addition to the Oaks, Portland had three others: Council Crest, Jantzen Beach, and Lotus Isle. (OHS neg. OrHi 26133)

Mary Dodge founded the Sagebrush Orchestra (pictured here) in Burns in the early years of this century. By 1915, her thirty-five member group of children was giving classical concerts throughout eastern Oregon and the Willamette Valley. Dodge went on with Jacques Gershkovitch to found the renowned Portland Youth Philharmonic. (OHS neg. OrHi 59409)

Harvey Scott, who came to Oregon in 1852, was editor of the *Oregonian* for nearly half a century. Though authoritarian, opinionated, and intensely conservative, Scott knew his Milton and his Burke, Shakespeare and the Bible, and read widely in many fields. Through this background, he gave the paper a kind of breadth and style that compared more than favorably with many American dailies. (OHS neg. Oreg. 4391)

Oregon City prospered with the building of the woolen mill pictured here (right) in 1867, the first on the Pacific Coast. (C. E. Watkins photo. OHS neg. OrHi 2159160)

It is said the first Japanese to reside in Oregon worked as a lamp lighter in Portland in 1860. Somewhat later, a sea captain brought his Japanese bride to Oregon and, it is asserted, named the settlement he founded near Gresham in her honor, Orient. However, there was no substantial Japanese immigration to Oregon until the 1880s when a number came to work on railroad construction. Later, many became successful truck farmers in the Willamette and Hood River valleys. Pictured here are the Japanese immigrants Issei with their American born infant in 1915. (Thomas Cronise photo. OHS neg. CN 0118 G 015)

TRAIN HOLDUP AT SISKIYOU, OCTOBER 11, 1923. FOUR MEN KILLED.

REWARD

OF

$4800.00

For Arrest and Conviction of Each Man

At least three implicated. Below are photographs and descriptions of two of three brothers wanted in connection with the holdup. Should be arrested on sight and held incommunicado.

Wire information, charges collect, to D. O'Connell, Chief Special Agent, Southern Pacific Railroad Company, or to C. Riddiford, Post Office Inspector in Charge, Ashland, Oregon, or to C. E. Terrill, Sheriff, Jackson County, at Medford, Oregon.

No. 1. Roy DeAutremont

Age: 23 years
Weight: 135 to 140 lbs.
Hair: Medium light, bleached by sun
Height: 5 ft. 6 inches
Complexion: Sandy
Eyes: Light brown. Small. Wears glasses at times, and eyes appear granulated and squinty.
Face broad, short cut neck, long nose and prominent nostrils
Face smooth. No marks. Head round
Twin brother of Number Two.

No. 2. Ray DeAutremont

Age: 23 years
Height: 5 ft. 6 inches
Weight: 135 to 140 lbs.
Complexion: Sandy
Hair as shown in Number one.
Broad face, short cut neck, face smooth.
Eyes: Light brown and small.
Twin brother of Number One.

No. 3. Hugh DeAutremont, alias E. E. James

Age: 19—Looks older
Height: 5 ft. 7 inches
Weight: 135 lbs.
Complexion: Fair
Eyes: Blue
Nose: Slightly pug

Hair: Medium light, slightly sandy and curly
Smooth shaven, wore short teet rain coat; also had mackinaw, but don't know what color
Brother of Numbers One and Two.

No. 4. Barnard LeChance

Age: About 30 years
Height: 5 ft. 8 inches
Weight: 150 lbs.

Hair: Black, large quantity of hair
Small black mustache
Is known as a Radical and Organizer.

MEDFORD PRINTING CO.

In October 1923, the three DeAutremont brothers, in what was called the nation's last great train robbery, dynamited the Southern Pacific's Gold Special when it passed through a tunnel in the Siskiyou Mountains near Ashland. In fact, the train carried no gold. Four trainmen were killed, but the brothers escaped into the mountains and were not captured until four years later. It was Oregon's most sensational criminal case. (OHS neg. OrHi 67257)

Born in Texas in 1889, Beatrice Morrow Cannady attended various schools in the South and Middlewest, including the University of Chicago, before coming to Portland where, in 1912, she began her distinguished career as an editor for the *Advocate*, the city's principal black newspaper. After attending the Northwest College of Law, she was admitted to the Oregon Bar in 1922, one of the first women attorneys in the Northwest. Mrs. Cannady was particularly active in promoting inter-racial understanding and furthering the careers of black artists. (OHS neg. CN 011493)

Radio station KGW began broadcasting from Portland in 1922, the first commercial station in Oregon. Here, Ronald G. Calvert, the station manager in 1925, listens to a broadcast. (OHS neg. OrHi 82066)

railroad. In 1906, Portland grudgingly raised the speed limit from eight to ten miles per hour. The real breakthrough came in 1910 when the Meier and Frank Company switched from horse delivery to trucks. In the same year, the Oregon Automobile Association called on the counties to put up road signs "so that autotourists . . . might be able to find their way anywhere in Oregon." It was now, too, the "good roads movement" increased its activity with its slogan, "Get Oregon out of the mud." In 1919, the state published its first official road map.

The canoe, the horse, the river boat, the stagecoach, even the railroads, impinged lightly on the Oregon landscape whereas the impact of the automobile was major. Among its many other effects, it continued and greatly augmented what the railroads had helped to begin: the gradual urbanization of the state. In 1890, only twenty-seven percent of the population lived in towns, in 1910, forty-six percent. According to the 1990 census, seventy-one percent of Oregonians live in towns and cities.

In addition to these important developments in the first years of the twentieth century—the reform movement, the growth and increasing urbanization of the population, the building of more and better roads—there was another that from then till now has been a prime determinant of the state's economic health: lumbering. A lumber mill was built by Dr. McLoughlin at Oregon City in 1831. With the gold rush, lumber became the state's principal export. Thereafter, the industry went into decline until the turn of the century and the depletion of eastern forests. The industry continued to grow, and in 1938, Oregon became the major lumber state in the nation.

By the time of World War I, the reform movement had pretty well petered out though Oregon continued to send reform-minded senators to Washington, men like Harry Lane and Charles McNary. As for the war itself, Oregon's response was whole-hearted. In keeping with the Spanish-American War record established by the "tall men of Oregon," Portland's National Guard unit was the first in the nation to mobilize, and Oregon as a whole, due to the extraordinary number of volunteers, became known as "the volunteer state."

As is so often the case, however, the coin of patriotism had its other side. Vigilante groups prowled Portland and other towns in search of dissidents. Pacifists refusing to buy war bonds were roughly treated. Even German street names were changed to the names of presidents and flowers.

Certain elements of the war years carried over into the next decade. The wartime shipyards did much to stimulate the timber trade, while war needs greatly increased food production and processing. Both industries contributed significantly to the prosperity of the state during the 1920s, but the intolerance of the war years extended into the decade as well. The Portland Police Department created a "Red Squad" that, in its enthusiasm, tended on occasion to overlook the law. Anti-Japanese sentiment surfaced in Klamath Falls, Redmond, and Hood River. The flaming crosses of the Ku Klux Klan flared from many a hill and butte. In the end, discriminatory legislation was passed adversely affecting Asians and Roman Catholics. It was an unlovely combination, the bigotry and boom.

The following decade brought some unlovely combinations, too: desperate men, frightened women, hungry children. Oregon was not as afflicted as many other states by the Depression, less dependent as it was on such hard-hit industries as automotives, steel, and textiles. Nonetheless Oregon, too, had its soup kitchens and Hoovervilles and Civilian Conservation Corps (CCC) camps. On the docks and in the logging camps there were bitter and violent labor disputes. The numbers of unemployed were increased as well by the arrival of migrants from the dustbowl states and the South—a new admixture to the Oregon population. In 1934, Governor Julius Meier summed up the general situation: "Oregon is dead broke."

As elsewhere, we grasped at panaceas such as the Townsend Plan and Technocracy. In 1937, however, a true if partial panacea did appear: Bonneville Dam. A cheap and plentiful source of power, it would, in time, have a profound effect on the character of the state's economy.

True economic revival did not occur until World War II. As in World War I, shipbuilding, lumber, and food production were greatly stimulated, and now, too, a new industry came to Oregon: aluminum. The war also brought new additions to Oregon's population, drawing 160,000 workers to the war industries. Among these came a large number of blacks, giving to the state for the first time a black population of significant size. Likewise, changing conditions in food production and crop harvesting offered jobs to Spanish-speaking migrants, many of whom settled and who now constitute the state's largest minority. The effect of the war on the character of Oregon's population and economy was to be both profound and lasting.

[*continued on page* 108]

Oregon has been building water craft since settlement. The first were the superb dugout canoes of the native Oregonians. Then, in 1811, the Astorians assembled a schooner, the *Dolly*, at Astoria. In the following decades, both ocean and river craft were built in great numbers on the coast and along the Columbia and Willamette rivers. The apex of Oregon shipbuilding, however, occurred in the Portland yards during the first and second world wars. (OHS neg. OrHi 12250)

Saloons and pool halls, despite condemnation by some, were popular places of resort for Oregon males. (OHS neg. OrHi 28889)

As this photo taken at Multnomah Falls reveals, at one point in our state's history public transport discriminated between smokers and ladies. (OHS neg. Gi 13035)

Everyone pitched in to help the war effort. (OHS neg. OrHi 82321)

The first Oregon State Fair (right) was held in 1866. Its purpose is to exhibit and award prizes to the blessings of the Oregon harvest—the animals, grains, grasses, vegetables, flowers, berries, and seeds, as well as all the products these afford. The fair also provides information on the latest agricultural and domestic science practices. Finally, the eleven-day gathering offers a full program of entertainment. The Oregon State Fair, held in Salem, is the state's single largest event. Pictured is a parade of livestock at the fair in 1936. (OHS neg. OrHi 82320)

The Civilian Conserva-
tion Corps (CCC) was a
federal program created
to provide employment
during the Depression.
Oregon parks owe much
to the Corps in construct-
ing trails, bridges, shel-
ters, picnic areas, and
campgrounds. Many
recruits remained in
Oregon after their
service. Pictured here are
CCC men of the Brice
Creek camp in Lane
County. (OHS neg. OrHi
53059)

Compared with many states, there has been little labor strife in Oregon, and the strikes have often been settled amicably. This seems to have been the case with the longshoremen's strike of 1937—at least from the point of view of the longshoremen pictured here at the Blue Bell Tavern in Portland. (*Oregon Journal* photo. OHS neg. OrHi 27630)

The first known Hispanics in Oregon history were the great seventeenth- and eighteenth-century maritime explorers, such as de Aguilar and Hezeta. However, Hispanics in numbers did not figure in the Oregon population until the 1920s, when they arrived from Mexico as migrant farm workers. Now, many Hispanics reside in Oregon and are in fact the state's largest minority. (OHS neg. OrHi 81788)

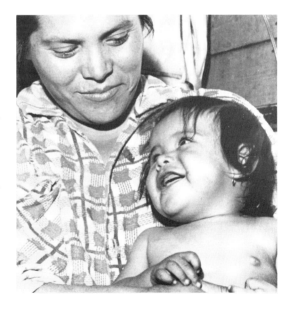

106

The first of the great Columbia River dams, Bonneville was completed in 1938. It was named for Captain Benjamin Bonneville, an army officer and explorer of western America. This dam and the later Columbia dams, as well as the irrigation and cheap power they provided, have had a profound effect on of the Northwest. (OHS neg. OrHi 42403)

A trio of eastern Oregonians discuss the world and its ways. (Lon Levy photo. OHS neg. OrHi 82322)

107

One element of the population that paradoxically remained alien among the rest were the native Oregonians, though in the first decades of the century certain advances were made. In 1924, the natives were finally made full citizens of the United States. In 1934, the Indian Reorganization Act provided for tribal councils and prohibited the sale of Indian lands to non-Indians. A decade later, a court of treaty claims was established. In the 1950s and early 1960s, however, the government—operating on the premise the natives should be assimilated into white society—terminated three Oregon reservations. The results on the whole did not contribute to the natives' welfare. By the late 1960s, perhaps in reaction to the dispersion caused by termination, there was a revival of tribalism. At the same time, government policy began to provide for self-determination, with lessened government and bureau influence in tribal affairs.

Today there are nine land-based tribal governments in Oregon: Burns Paiute Tribe; The Klamath Tribes; Confederated Tribes of the Warm Springs Reservation; Confederated Tribes of the Umatilla Indian Reservation; Confederated Tribes of the Coos, Lower Umpqua and Siuslaw Indians; Coquille Indian Tribe; Cow Creek Band of Umpqua Indians; Confederated Tribes of Grand Ronde; and Confederated Tribes of Siletz. Each tribe is recognized as having inherent rights and a trust relationship with the United States government. The present policy regarding Native People in Oregon and their plans for the future is noted in the 1983 OHS publication, *Oregon Indians: Culture, History and Current Affairs.*

> The continuing acknowledgment of tribal sovereignty and the support for self-determination is a policy approach that rests solidly on the most basic points of Indian and United States legal history, and it holds much promise for the future. It may be that now, after more than two centuries, the right of Indian people to live their own lives, and determine their own destiny, will finally be respected.

108

8
A Time-Deep Land

As with any object held too close, the recent past is difficult to see, events in postwar Oregon still too near to be perceived with true perspective. Still, from the present vantage point, there are certain events and trends that would appear to be of permanent significance.

Oregon's economy continues to depend heavily on lumber and agriculture. Two new industries, however, have broadened the economic base: electronics and tourism. Oregon is an ideal location for the former because the electronics industry is not dependent upon raw materials or close proximity to markets but, on the other hand, does require the skilled labor force Oregon can provide. Tourism, only recently thought of as an industry, has vastly increased since the war and is now the state's third largest source of revenue. Both electronics and tourism are fortunate new directions for the state's economy since neither threatens Oregon's most important resource after its people—the land on which they live.

Another departure is the state's new political complexion. For the first time in nearly a century, the Democrats came to be the majority party, though important offices continue to be held by Republicans. In part, this Democratic majority is due to the numbers of war workers who remained on to settle. It can also be attributed to the predominantly Democratic affiliation of the large influx of easterners from the 1950s through the 1970s. At the state level, political activity has been greatly concerned with environmental legislation, though with bipartisan support. As at the beginning of the century, when Oregon led the nation with the Oregon System of legislative reform, so in the area of environmental protection it has taken the lead with such citizen-supported measures as the Scenic Rivers Act, the Land Conservation and Development Commission (LCDC), and the Bottle Bill. The first settlers believed Oregon to be an Eden. Now, a century and a half later, their descendants appear determined to see that it remains so.

Driving down the roads of Oregon today, whether in the Valley, the interior, or the coast, and looking at the landscape and all the things so recently put upon it, it is easy to forget it all began more than ten thousand years ago when the land came to rest and humans arrived to live from it. Cruising the freeway hardly brings to mind those first one hundred centuries of native life, only in detail different from our own, at bottom the same: shelter, food, some ornament and myth, birth, growing, and decay. History, it is said, is a pageant, a procession that never pauses, both the figures and the backdrops always changing. Thus, with the long, slow centuries of native life did the pageant of Oregon begin.

Processions, though they never pause, do proceed at different rates—the rate in history determined by the rate of change—and so it is that the pageant of Oregon's history begins to quicken with the first appearance off the coast of those great black-bodied birds, the ships of the explorers. Hezeta retiring, disappointed, from the mouth of the Columbia; Gray, triumphant, crashing through the breakers at the bar; Lewis and Clark, waterborne as well, celebrating Christmas with "Spoiled Pounded fish and a fiew roots."

The backdrop changes to Fort Vancouver and Dr. McLoughlin belaboring his cane on someone's back or holding up that goblet of port to the sunlight, while thirty miles along the Willamette the French Canadian trappers with their Indian mates are sowing wheat and children. Enter the grave, dedicated missionaries, their faces finally cast with bafflement and failure; followed by the immigrants, "lank, lean and tough." They are best backdropped by the falls at Oregon City where most of them arrived, or searching for claims in the mud of the Oregon winter. Next, there is a confusion of gold and blood, Indian wars and miners, and at the same time, someone burns down the statehouse, and both Whigs and Democrats are hanged in effigy. Meanwhile, the general background of all of this—the long, green valley with its meander of river—is filling up with houses,

110

barns, churches, schoolhouses, taverns, shops, and here and there a huddle of them, the largest huddle of all at the last bend of the Willamette.

No sooner has one begun to take in all of this than the backdrop begins to broaden. At the top appears a scene half plain, half sky, vast herds of cattle moving through it, soon to dwindle as the green of grazing passes to the gold of wheat, while at the bottom, little lighthouses go up at the ends of the headlands, and the natives lose their land and die.

For some time it has been a noisy pageant—laughter, gunfire, war whoops, the intoning of sermons, a politician's blast, the cries of love and pain, ironshod wheels on cobblestones—all in all a terrible racket. But now there comes a sound that splits the air like the bugles of perdition, except it is a whistle. The railroad has arrived.

From now on, the speed of the procession is such that one can hardly keep up with it. Wheat pours down on Portland. New towns are built. A horde of immigrants descend. The people capture the statehouse. Women get the vote. The automobile appears. And before we know it, we are flying down the freeway, gazing out across this time-deep land where, as we sometimes forget, so much has happened.

Chronological History of Oregon

OREGON COUNTRY 1542-1847

1542-43   Bartolomé Ferrelo, pilot for Juan Rodríguez Cabrillo, sails north as far as the southern coast of Oregon in the vicinity of the Rogue River.

1579   Sir Francis Drake sails north to the southern coast of Oregon.

1600s   Galleon trade begins between Spain's new possessions in the Philippines and Mexico.

1603   Martín de Aguilar sails along the Oregon coast and sights evidence of a river where the Columbia is later discovered.

1707   The *San Francisco Xavier* wrecks at the base of Neahkahnie Mountain on Oregon's coast.

1765   "Ouragon," first known use of Oregon, is called so by Major Robert Rogers.

1774   Juan Pérez sails along the Oregon coast, first known Spanish explorer in 170 years.

1775   Bruno de Hezeta and Juan Francisco de Bodega y Quadra land on what is now the Washington shore. They are the first known Europeans to stand on Northwest soil.

1778	Captain James Cook visits the Northwest Coast on a voyage of discovery and through his sea otter trade with China, starts heavy fur trading with many nations in the Pacific Northwest.
	John Meares sails by the mouth of the Columbia River, but not crediting the river's existence, he names its estuary Deception Bay.
1779	First white men, American seamen, land on Oregon shores from the *Lady Washington*.
	"Oregon" is first used in print by Jonathan Carver.
1787	Pacific Triangular Trade is born.
1788	Captain Robert Gray lands on the Oregon coast near present Tillamook—the first American to do so. He bargains with the natives for sea otter pelts which he then trades in the Orient before returning to Boston as the first American to circumnavigate the globe.
1792	Captain Robert Gray discovers the River of the West, which he names the Columbia after his ship, the *Columbia Rediviva*. George Vancouver unknowingly sails past the mouth of the Columbia earlier in the year.
	Lieutenant William Broughton, of Vancouver's crew, spends three weeks on the Columbia investigating the interior.
1793	In what is now British Columbia, Sir Alexander Mackenzie canoes down the Bella Coola River to the Pacific Ocean. He is the first white man to cross the North American continent.
1803	President Jefferson purchases Louisiana from France. American interests now turn to this new land of Louisiana and the unknown wilderness beyond it called the Oregon Country.
1804-06	Captains Lewis and Clark and their party travel from St. Louis to the mouth of the Columbia River.
1807-12	A North West Company British fur trader and explorer, David Thompson, travels the entire length of the Columbia River. He is the first white man to do so.

1811	The Pacific Fur Company is established near the mouth of the Columbia River where Astoria now stands. John Jacob Astor finances this enterprise.
1812	South Pass, the gateway through the Rocky Mountains, is discovered by Robert Stuart of the Pacific Fur Company. South Pass is later used by pioneers on the Oregon Trail.
1813	The Pacific Fur Company agrees to sell its outpost at Astoria to the North West Company, a British fur-trading enterprise. Considered a prize of the War of 1812, possession of the fort is taken by the British in 1814. It is then renamed Fort George.
1814	Jane Barnes, first white woman to land in the Pacific Northwest, arrives at Fort George by ship.
	First livestock in the Pacific Northwest are brought from California by ship.
1818	Fort George nominally returns to American ownership by the Treaty of 1814. A treaty of joint occupancy is signed by the United States and Great Britain for this Pacific Northwest territory.
1821	North West Company merges with Hudson's Bay Company.
1824	Hudson's Bay Company headquarters in the Pacific Northwest are moved from Fort George to the newly selected Fort Vancouver site on the north bank of the Columbia River (the fort is dedicated in 1825). Dr. John McLoughlin becomes chief factor at the post, where he remains for twenty-two years.
1827	First sawmill in the Pacific Northwest is built by Dr. McLoughlin.
1828	Jedediah Smith, a fur trapper, reaches the Pacific Northwest from California. His is the first party to travel overland from California. Fifteen of his eighteen men are killed by Indians along the Umpqua River.

1828	First grist mills are built by the Hudson's Bay Company at Fort Vancouver and Fort Colville.
1829	Dr. John McLoughlin establishes a town at Willamette Falls, the present site of Oregon City.
	McLoughlin allows French Canadian trappers to settle along the banks of the Willamette River near present St. Paul.
1831	Four Oregon Country Indians travel to St. Louis seeking missionaries to come to the region.
1832	Captain Benjamin Bonneville and a party of 110 men come west via the Rocky Mountains and travel to Fort Walla Walla.
	Nathaniel Wyeth's first expedition travels into the Columbia River country.
	Hudson's Bay Company establishes a fort on the Umpqua River.
1833	Methodist divine, Wilbur Fisk, urges missionaries to go to Oregon to spread the word of Christ to the natives.
	First school in the Pacific Northwest is established at Fort Vancouver. The school's teacher, John Ball, was a member of Nathaniel Wyeth's party.
	First timber shipment from Oregon is sent to China.
1834	Fort Hall, in what is now Idaho, is established by Nathaniel Wyeth on his second expedition.
	Jason Lee party of the first Protestant missionaries to the Oregon Country arrives at Fort Vancouver with Nathaniel Wyeth. The Lees later establish the Willamette Mission near present Salem.
1836	*The Beaver*, first steamboat on the Pacific Ocean, is brought to Fort Vancouver.
	Protestant missionaries, Dr. Marcus Whitman, H. H. Spalding, their wives, and W. H. Gray, arrive in the Oregon

Country. Narcissa Whitman and Eliza Spalding are the first white women to come across the continent to the Oregon Country. This is also the first group to bring wagons west of Fort Hall.

Waiilatpu Mission is established by Dr. Whitman. Alice Clarissa, the Whitmans' daughter, is the first white American child born in the region.

1838   Missionaries plant the seed of statehood as Jason Lee carries a memorial to the nation's capital asking Congress to extend United States jurisdiction over Oregon.

Fathers Francis Norbert Blanchet and Modeste Demers celebrate the first Roman Catholic mass in the Pacific Northwest.

First cattle drive of the West arrives from California.

1839   First printing press in the Northwest is brought to Lapwai (now Idaho) from Honolulu and is used to print a Nez Perce primer, the first book published in the Pacific Northwest.

Father Blanchet establishes the first Roman Catholic mission in what is now St. Paul, Oregon.

1841   American settlers in the Willamette Valley meet to create a government but fail.

The *Star of Oregon*, first ship built by Americans in the Oregon Country, is launched.

1842   Dr. John McLoughlin designs plans for what is now Oregon City.

Willamette University, the first university west of the Mississippi River, is founded by Jason Lee.

1843   Civil government is established in the Oregon Country.

First large group of Americans arrives over the Oregon Trail; approximately nine hundred settle in the Willamette Valley.

1844   National election slogan "54-40 or Fight" proves growing American interest in Oregon.

First American taxes on the Pacific Coast are collected on a voluntary basis.

1845   Second provisional government in Oregon Country is organized. George Abernethy is elected provisional governor.

Portland has its humble beginning—sixteen blocks platted along the Willamette River.

1846   Treaty between the United States and Great Britain establishes the Oregon boundary at forty-nine degrees north latitude.

Dr. John McLoughlin resigns from his post as chief factor for the Hudson's Bay Company at Fort Vancouver. He retires to the town he founded, Oregon City.

First newspaper, the *Oregon Spectator*, is published at Oregon City.

1847   Whitman Massacre at Waiilatpu (Cayuse War, the first Oregon Country Indian war, follows).

OREGON TERRITORY 1848-58

1848   Oregon Territory is organized on 14 August. (Abraham Lincoln is asked to be governor of the Territory of Oregon).

A Captain Newell sails up the Willamette River buying spades, picks, and shovels. He then informs the locals that gold has been discovered in California. An estimated two-thirds of able-bodied Oregonians leave for the gold fields of California.

1849   General Joseph Lane, first appointed territorial governor and first superintendent of Indian affairs, arrives.

Vancouver is made military headquarters for the Pacific Northwest.

1850   Donation Land Claim law is enacted.

Mail service between San Francisco and the Columbia River is established.

1850s   More than thirty towns are registered in the Willamette Valley, and fourteen steamboats make scheduled runs on the Willamette River.

1851   Portland is incorporated (named after Portland, Maine, by flipping a coin to decide between the names of Boston and Portland).

1853   Washington Territory is created from part of the Oregon Territory. Southern boundary is marked by the Columbia River.

Joel Palmer takes office as superintendent of Indian affairs and later initiates the reservation system in Oregon to protect the natives.

Labor organization begins in Oregon with the creation of the Typographical Society.

1853-56 Rogue River Indian wars.

1855   The Yakima Indian War begins. It is fought on both sides of the mid-Columbia River.

First telegraph company is operated in Oregon.

1856   Portions of eastern Washington and Oregon are closed to settlers by Army order, due to Indian war.

1858   Oregon holds first election of state officers.

1859 Congress ratifies Oregon State Constitution (14 February). This is the formal birthday of the state.

Congressional proposal to admit Oregon to the Union is accepted by the state (3 June).

John Whiteaker becomes the first elected governor of Oregon.

Ladd and Tilton Bank, first in the state, is founded.

1860 Daily stagecoach service is inaugurated between Portland and Sacramento.

1861-62 Gold strikes in Baker and Grant counties help set off the interior's "gold, grass and grain" years.

Cattle drives across the Cascades from the Willamette Valley begin.

1863 Idaho Territory is created. Eventually, three states are created from the original Oregon Country.

Fort Stevens is built on the Columbia and becomes the principal guardian of the river for eighty-four years.

1864 Salem becomes the state capital by popular vote.

Transcontinental telegraph lines into Portland via California are in place.

First salmon canning factory is established at Astoria.

1866 Regular stage runs begin on the new military road from Corvallis to Newport where the Ocean House, a resort hotel, is built.

1868 Corvallis College (now, Oregon State University) is designated as the Agricultural College of Oregon, the first state-supported institution of higher education in Oregon.

1869 First public high school is established in Oregon.

First wheat shipment from Portland goes to Liverpool.

120

1870s	Oregon Grange begins the first protests of high freight rates.
1872	Modoc Indian War.
	Portland is linked with Roseburg by rail.
1876	State capitol is built.
	University of Oregon is established in Eugene.
1877	Nez Perce Indian War.
1878	Bannock Indian War.
1882	State normal schools for training teachers are established at Monmouth and Ashland.
1883	Transcontinental railroad is completed.
1886	Populist candidate Sylvestor Pennoyer is elected to the governorship—reform achieves a significant victory.
1887	Oregon-California railroad is completed.
	American Federation of Labor is formed.
	Dawes Act abolishes the Indians' communal ownership of their reservation. Instead, they are given individual parcels of land to encourage independent farming. The act greatly reduces the amount of Indian-held land.
1887-90s	Local railroad lines are constructed to the coast, the interior, and throughout the Willamette Valley. The railroads strengthen Portland's dominance of the state's interior.
1898	Oregon Volunteer group is part of the first military expedition to the Philippines.
	Progressive W. S. U'Ren and Direct Legislation League take power—political corruption is suppressed.
1902	Initiative and referendum laws are adopted allowing the people of Oregon to place measures on the ballot and to recall existing laws by popular vote. Oregon is the first state to adopt such laws.

1905   Lewis and Clark Centennial Exposition is held in Portland, celebrating one hundred years since the arrival of the explorers in the region.

1906   Portland raises its speed limit from eight to ten miles per hour.

1910   Meier and Frank stores switch from horse delivery to trucks.

Oregon Automobile Association calls for counties to put up road signs.

The Good Road Movement spawns the slogan, "Get Oregon Out of the Mud."

1912   Woman suffrage is adopted in Oregon.

1913   South jetty at the mouth of the Columbia River is completed to facilitate shipping on the Columbia and Willamette rivers.

Workers Compensation law is passed—the first effective minimum wage/maximum hour law for women in the nation.

1918   Portland's National Guard units are the first in the nation to mobilize for World War I. The same patriotic spirit sparks vigilante groups to prowl Portland and other towns in search of dissidents.

1919   Oregon's first official road map is published.

1920s   Portland Police Department creates a "Red Squad," and discriminatory legislation is passed adversely affecting Orientals and Roman Catholics.

1922   Compulsory education law is passed.

1924   Oregon Indians are granted full United States citizenship.

1933   The Tillamook Burn, one of the nation's worst forest disasters, wipes out 240,000 acres of Oregon's finest timber.

The Coast Highway is completed.

1934   Indian Reorganization Act is passed.

1935   State capitol is destroyed by fire.

1938   Bonneville Dam is completed, providing Oregon with a great source of hydroelectric power.

Oregon becomes the major lumber state in the nation.

1939   New capitol in Salem is completed.

1941   Shipbuilding boom starts in Portland.

1945   Aluminum industry begins in Oregon.

One hundred sixty thousand workers are drawn to the war industries in the state, including Oregon's first substantial black population. Large numbers of Spanish-speaking immigrants come to work in Oregon's growing food industry.

1946   Act creates Indian Claims Commission.

1947   Governor Earl Snell, Secretary of State Robert S. Farrell, Jr., and President of Senate Marshall E. Cornett are killed in a private plane crash.

1948   Memorial Day flood completely destroys "Oregon's second-largest city," Vanport, a suburban Portland city built to house war-time workers.

1949   Fair Employment Practices Commission, the first in a series of state civil rights legislation, is established.

1952   Constitutional amendment is approved assuring equal representation in State Legislature.

1954   McNary Dam on the Columbia River is dedicated by President Dwight D. Eisenhower.

1959   Oregon celebrates its centennial birthday (14 February).

1961   Freeway is completed connecting Salem and Portland.

1962   "Columbus Day" (12 October) storm causes extensive damage.

1964	Christmas flood inundates large portions of Oregon.
1966	Astoria bridge linking Oregon and Washington at the mouth of the Columbia River is open.
	Ceremony marking completion of Interstate 5 freeway takes place.
1967	Beach Bill is approved.
1968	John Day Dam, on the Columbia River, is dedicated by Vice-President Hubert Humphrey.
1971	Bottle Bill is approved, the first in the nation.
	Single member district reapportionment is established for the Oregon Legislature.
1973	Statewide land use planning is approved.
	Equal Rights Amendment (ERA) to the United States Constitution is ratified and reaffirmed in 1977.
1977	Ban on aerosol sprays goes into effect on 1 March.
	State Capitol Wings addition is completed.
1980	Mt. St. Helens erupts with cataclysmic force in southwestern Washington, devastating two hundred square miles of popular forestland and triggering destructive ash, floods, mud flows, and river silt. The busy Columbia River is temporarily closed to deep-draft ships at Portland and Vancouver.
1981	Oregon unemployment is at 11.1 percent, the highest since the Great Depression of the 1930s.
1982	Cow Creek Band of Upper Umpqua Indians win restoration of trust relationship.
	Betty Roberts is the first woman justice of the Supreme Court of Oregon.
1983	Confederated Tribes of Grand Ronde win restoration of trust relationship.

1984	Confederated Tribes of Coos, Lower Umpqua and Siuslaw Indians win restoration of trust relationship.
	Voters approve both the lottery and the death penalty.
1985	Vera Katz, a Democrat, becomes the first woman speaker of the Oregon House of Representatives.
	Rajneeshpuram declines after the arrest of Indian guru Bhagwan Shree Rajneesh.
1986	Klamath Tribe wins restoration of trust relationship.
	China Gateway, the second largest in the United States, is dedicated in Portland.
	Seven students and two teachers die in a Mt. Hood blizzard.
1987	Fires burn 245,000 acres of timber worth an estimated $97.3 million.
	Oregon Vietnam Veterans Living Memorial dedicated in Portland.
1988	State Capitol is fifty years old, officially listed in Historic Register.
1990	The Northern Spotted Owl listed as a threatened species by the U.S. Department of Fish and Wildlife.
	Voters pass Ballot Measure 5, limiting property taxes for schools and government operations.
1991	Barbara Roberts inaugurated as Oregon's first woman governor.
1992	James A. Hill, Jr. elected as first black state official.
1993	Oregon Trail 150th Anniversary Celebration.
	Oregon holds the nation's first statewide vote-by-mail election.
1995	Bev Clarno becomes first Republican woman to serve as speaker of the Oregon House of Representatives.

1996   Oregon conducts the nation's first vote-by-mail election for a federal office.

Douglas Franklin Wright executed at the Oregon State Penitentiary—the state's first in thirty-four years.

Selected Bibliography

GENERAL

Bancroft, Hubert Howe. *History of Oregon*, 2 volumes, San Francisco: The History Company, 1886-88.

Dodds, Gordon B. *The American Northwest: A History of Oregon and Washington*, Arlington Heights, Illinois: Forum Press, 1986.

1 *Figures in the Dawn*

Ramsey, Jarold, ed., comp. *Coyote Was Going There: Indian Literature of the Oregon Country*, Seattle: University of Washington Press, 1977.

Zucker, Jeff, Bob Høgfoss, Kay Hummel. *Oregon Indians: Culture, History and Current Affairs: An Atlas and Introduction*, Portland, Oregon: Oregon Historical Society Press, 1983.

2 *Landfalls & Forest Trails*

De Voto, Bernard, ed. *The Journals of Lewis and Clark*, Boston: Houghton Mifflin, 1953.

Pethic, Derek. *First Approaches to the Northwest Coast*, Vancouver, B.C.: J. J. Douglas, Ltd., 1976.

3 *Beavers & Bibles*

Jones, Nard. *The Great Command: The Story of Marcus and Narcissa Whitman and the Oregon Country Pioneers*, Boston: Little, Brown, 1959. (A novel)

Lavender, David. *The First in the Wilderness*, Albuquerque: University of New Mexico Press, 1964.

Loewenberg, Robert J. *Equality on the Oregon Frontier: Jason Lee and the Methodist Mission, 1834-43*, Seattle: University of Washington Press, 1976.

Victor, Frances Fuller. *The River of the West*, Columbus, Ohio: Long's College Book Co., 1950.

4 *Eden Seekers*

Guthrie, Alfred Bertram. *The Way West*, New York: W. Sloane Associates, 1949. (A novel)

Unruh, Jr., John David. *The Plains Across: The Overland Emigrants and the Trans-Mississippi West, 1840-60*, Urbana, Illinois: University of Illinois Press, 1979.

5 *Decade of Decisions*

Clark, Malcolm. *Eden Seekers: The Settlement of Oregon, 1818-1862*, Boston: Houghton Mifflin, 1981.

Nunis, Jr., Doyce B., ed. *The Golden Frontier: The Recollections of Herman Francis Reinhart, 1851-69*, Austin: University of Texas Press, 1962.

O'Donnell, Terence. *An Arrow in the Earth: General Joel Palmer and the Indians of Oregon*, Portland, Oregon: Oregon Historical Society Press, 1991.

Victor, Frances Fuller. *The Early Indian Wars of Oregon*, Salem, Oregon: F. C. Baker, 1894.

6 *The Valley & Beyond*

Berry, Don. *Trask*, New York: Viking Press, 1960. (A novel)

Bowen, William A. *The Willamette Valley: Migration and Settlement on the Oregon Frontier*, Seattle: University of Washington Press, 1979.

Meinig, Donald W. *The Great Columbia Plain: A Historical Geography, 1805-1910,* Seattle: University of Washington Press, 1968.

Throckmorton, Arthur L. *Oregon Argonauts: Merchant Adventurers on the Western Frontier*, Portland, Oregon: Oregon Historical Society Press, 1961.

7 *Passing of the Past*

Bone, Arthur H., ed. *Oregon Cattleman, Governor, Congressman: Memoirs and Times of Walter M. Pierce,* Portland, Oregon: Oregon Historical Society Press, 1981.

Culp, Edwin D. *Stations West: The Story of the Oregon Railroads,* Caldwell, Idaho: The Caxton Printers, Ltd., 1972.

Davis, Harold L. *Honey in the Horn*, New York: Harper and Brothers, 1935. (A novel)

Drukman, Mason. *Wayne Morse: A Political Biography*, Portland, Oregon: Oregon Historical Society Press, 1997.

Lucia, Ellis. *The Big Woods: Logging and Lumbering from Bull Teams to Helicopters in the Pacific Northwest*, Garden City, New York: Doubleday, Inc., 1975.

Moynihan, Ruth Barnes. *Rebel For Rights: Abigail Scott Duniway*, New Haven: Yale University Press, 1983.

Neal, Steve. *McNary of Oregon: A Political Biography*, Portland, Oregon: Oregon Historical Society Press, 1985.

Walth, Brent. *Fire at Eden's Gate: Tom McCall and the Oregon Story*, Portland, Oregon: Oregon Historical Society Press, 1994.

8 *A Time-Deep Land*

Edwards, G. Thomas and Carlos Schwantes. *Experiences in the Promised Land: Essays in Pacific Northwest History*, Seattle: University of Washington Press, 1986.

Vaughan, Thomas and Virginia G. Ferriday. *Space, Style and Structure: Buildings in Northwest America*, Portland, Oregon: Oregon Historical Society Press, 1974.

Vaughan, Thomas, ed. *The Western Shore: Oregon Country Essays Honoring the American Revolution*, Portland, Oregon: Oregon Historical Society Press, 1975.

Index

134

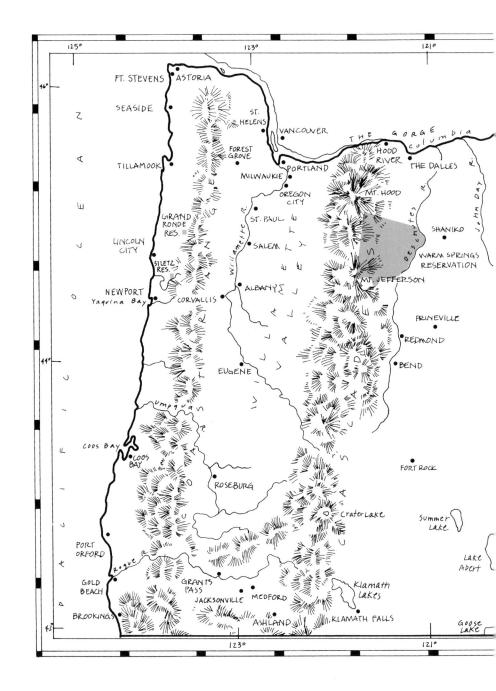

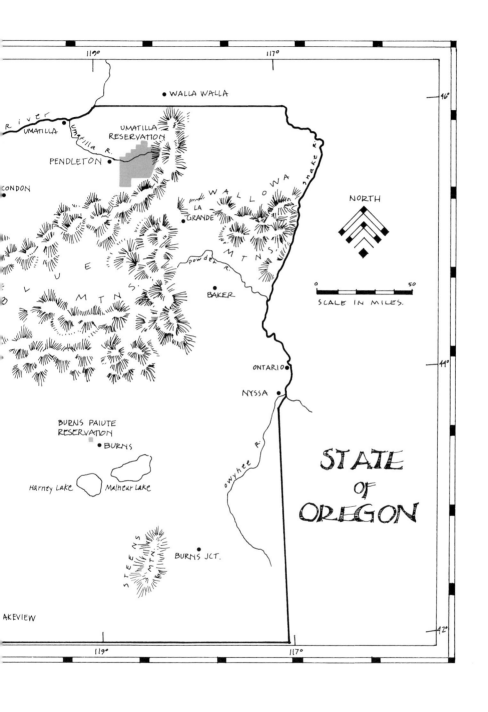

Colophon

That Balance So Rare is set in the Galliard typeface is is printed on 80 lb. Lustro Dull Cream.

Produced and designed by the Oregon Historical Society Press.

Production of this work was achieved through the expertise and cooperation of the following:

TYPESETTING:	Irish Setter
PRINTING:	Bang Printing
EDITING:	Lori McEldowney
INTERIOR DESIGN:	George Resch
COVER DESIGN:	Martha Gannett
MAPS:	Christine Rains